The Feminine Spirit

Recapturing the Heart of Scripture

The Woman's Guide to the Bible

Lynne Bundesen

John Wiley & Sons, Inc.

Published by Jossey-Bass
A Wiley Imprint
989 Market Street, San Francisco, CA 94103–1741   www.josseybass.com

Jossey-Bass books and products are available through most bookstores. To contact Jossey-Bass directly call our Customer Care Department within the U.S. at 800-956-7739, outside the U.S. at 317-572-3986, or fax 317-572-4002.

Jossey-Bass also publishes its books in a variety of electronic formats. Some content that appears in print may not be available in electronic books.

Library of Congress Cataloging-in-Publication Data
Bundesen, Lynne.
  The feminine spirit : recapturing the heart of scripture :
the woman's guide to the Bible / Lynne Bundesen.
      p. cm.
  Includes bibliographical references.
  ISBN-13: 978-0-7879-8495-3 (pbk.)
  ISBN-10: 0-7879-8495-7 (pbk.)
  1. Bible—Feminist criticism. I. Title.
  BS511.3.B86 2007
  220.6082—dc22   2006035829

Printed in the United States of America
FIRST EDITION
PB Printing 10 9 8 7 6 5 4 3 2 1

Contents

Note to the Reader

The Bible has a long history as the backdrop for domestic, national, and international relations. That history extends to our time.

This book traces two biblical themes. First, it offers a corrective and nondenominational reading of the Bible that has, by interpreters for centuries, traced an exclusively male God. This book looks at the textbook of current Western culture from interpretations of the Original Text and traces the biblical, textual narrative of a female-gendered Spirit, God.

Second, in the light of this female Spirit, this book looks at familiar accounts of the stories of women and men in the Bible and offers a view of their stories in the light of the female nature of God and how that view impacts lives today.

No previous Bible knowledge is required to read this book, but readers not familiar or well-acquainted with the Bible will find the introduction, Starting the Journey, particularly helpful. These few pages give useful pointers on reading the Bible and the various biblical translations and versions used in this Guide.

In my half a century of Bible study I have come to see the Bible as an elegant and practical unveiling of spiritual power for women as well as men. Alone and with teachers, with countless texts and commentaries, at home and across the globe, in study as well as teaching, I have found the Bible to be a companion and guide.

My purpose in writing this book is a hope that others may find, as I have, freshness and inspiration in a balanced, gendered reading of the most important book of our ages.

Starting the Journey:
How to Begin

What if the Bible were easy to read and—in just the turn of a page—you could find the comfort, inspiration, and answers you need today?

How can you read the Bible easily? Begin by reading the Bible as the woman or man you are today—as the sum of all your experience.

Take the Book, go into a room alone, and shut the door behind you. Or, if you prefer, take the Book and go out for a walk.

This simple approach is deliberate. The Bible becomes more immediate if you read it alone. No one hears with your ears, sees with your eyes, knows what you need, what you want, where you want to go in just the way that you do.

Allow yourself to be alone with the Bible and your own unlimited potential for understanding it. The Bible is a lens that magnifies your spiritual self. Reading glasses, mirrors, camera pictures, and the approval of friends are poor substitutes for the vision that exists when you see the Book as a guide to your own consciousness. A Bible of your own is the passport to the greatest adventure of all— the adventure toward self-realization. Each reader in each age is always discovering the Bible. You are on a voyage of discovery.

The Bible you choose should be one that is yours, that speaks in a language you appreciate. Choose the Bible that suits you, just as you choose the music you listen to in your most private, personal moments.

Translations

Unless you read Hebrew—the original language of the Jewish Bible—or the biblical Greek language of the New Testament, you will be reading a translation. Translations of the Bible exist not only in almost every spoken language on earth but often in many styles of just one of those languages. You will probably want to compare several different translations of the Bible to find one that most nearly fits your style. Some Bibles have many different translations all on the same page.[1]

Churches and religions use different translations of the Bible, depending on their traditions. But you are not a church or a religion. You are an individual about to begin reading the Bible as the person you are today. In this book you will see notations after Bible passages, citing chapter and verse. Unless otherwise indicated, the translation is from the King James Version, the most influential in the English language and the one on which many other translations are based. For those passages taken from other translations, there will be an abbreviation indicating the specific translation. Here are the standard abbreviations:

Alter	*The Five Books of Moses: A Translation with Commentary*
AT	*The Bible: An American Translation*
CEV	*The Bible for Today's Family: Contemporary English Version*
GNB	*The Good News Bible*
NAB	*New American Bible*
NIV	*Holy Bible: New International Version*
NJB	*The New Jerusalem Bible*
NRSV	*Holy Bible: New Revised Standard Version*
Peterson	*The Message: The Bible in Contemporary Language*
Phillips	*The New Testament in Modern English*

The Torah *The Torah: A Modern Commentary*

TNK   *Tanakh—The Holy Scriptures: The New JPS*
         Translation of the Holy Scriptures According to
         the Traditional Hebrew Text (JPS refers to Jewish
         Publication Society)

Tyndale *Tyndale's Old Testament*

Since the King James Version of the Bible was first published in 1611 and the Bible became available to the individual lay reader, the idea that God is male has informed literature, language, and national and international policies.[2]

Language conveys overt and hidden messages and forms the way we think. The idea that the biblical God is male has subjugated women, who are told the Bible says that they are property and that they must obey their husbands. What that false reading of the Bible's words has provoked for life on earth is beyond measure and comprehension. However, it is safe to say that the false reading that God is male has overturned the full biblical message, as you will discover as you read this book.

Reading for Yourself

This book will help you read the Bible for yourself and help you discover the female aspect of God, the Creator, God the Mother that already exists in the Book. To read the Bible as it is written, to appreciate the feminine aspect of the God of the Bible, may lead you to revise your view of God and of yourself. You will learn to easily translate for yourself the many aspects and biblical names of God already available to us in the original text. To follow the female Spirit of God through the Bible is not to change God, but to clarify our view, bringing freedom from past interpretations—stemming from a superficial reading of the text—that subjugate and exploit peoples.

For the purposes of this book, the Bible is taken as a whole and not as a denominational text, which will allow a reading of the themes and repeated words from Genesis to Revelation. Any reference to words or themes to come later is not an attempt to force a denomination on any of the biblical texts, nor is it an attempt to negate any particular manner of worship. For the purposes of this book, it is best to read the Bible as a whole for its inspiration—not to prove anyone right or wrong.

Pleasing a King

It is not just the translation of the Hebrew text, but also the tone of the translation in the King James Version that has led to confusion about the nature of the biblical God. In naming the translation after James I (1566–1625), king of England and Scotland, the translators were fully aware that James had earlier written for publication his view of the monarch as spiritual patriarch. It is no surprise that a magisterial, regal note crept into the translated King James Bible texts. This tone has come to represent what is referred to as "male thinking"—direct and to the point. Yet the original Hebrew biblical texts do not indicate this type of thinking. They indicate process, not fiat. The following texts show the difference that even a period—a full stop—brings to the tone and sense of the first verses of Genesis and perhaps to our sense of God.

Here is the King James translation:

In the beginning God created the heaven and the earth.

And the earth was without form, and void; and darkness was upon the face of the deep. And the Spirit of God moved upon the face of the waters.

And God said, Let there be light: and there was light.

And the Hebrew translation:

When God began to create heaven and earth—the earth being unformed and void, with darkness over the surface of the deep and a wind from God sweeping over the water—God said, "Let there be light"; and there was light. (TNK)

The King James translation starts with a pronouncement—a single declarative sentence. The new JPS translation from the traditional Hebrew text has Creation as process—not stopping until there is light. The Hebrew, the original language of Genesis, recounts the Beginning with several active elements—to be pondered and explored in subsequent chapters in this book.

The Hebrew Bible of thirty-nine books is divided into three parts: the Law, the Prophets, and the Writings. The New Testament has twenty-seven books. Christians who are Roman Catholics read seven additional books.

Like people, the Bible comes in all sizes and colors. The Bible is available in large type, small print, Braille, audiotapes, all styles of computer software, and on the Internet.

Go to a used bookstore, order a Bible through the mail, get one free from a Bible society, ask a friend to buy one for you, rummage through your great-aunt's belongings, borrow one from the library, or read one on the Internet. Or, when staying at any motel, take the Gideon Bible from the nightstand.

Yours Alone

Alone and comfortable, hold the Bible in your hands.

Open the book to any page.

You are looking for inspiration, not history. The Bible does not have to be read in chronological order.

Take two or three deep breaths.

Look down at the page and read something until it catches your eye or ear. Then, stop reading and remember the words that struck you or the question that was raised in your mind.

Be still for a few moments and listen quietly. Take time to reflect on the words, the images, and the thoughts that arise. What you are looking and listening for is not merely the literal interpretation but the spiritual.

Make a note of the verse or the words that caught your attention.

This is easy to do. Bibles have the name of the book at the top of every page. Your Bible should include a table of contents, indicating the page on which each book begins. Chapters are numbered, as are verses. For example, when you read Genesis 1:1, you know you are in the Book of Genesis, first chapter, first verse. All Bibles use the same chapter and verse markings.

The chapter and verse references in this book are noted. Don't feel that you necessarily have to look up each and every reference any more than you would have to visit each and every town on a map. But, as with a map, at least you know where places are located in the overall scheme of the territory. And should you want to visit particular places, you know where to go and how to get there. Before you have traveled any distance at all in this book you will know how to find for yourself anything or any place in your Bible.

Variety of Biblical Texts

There are wonderful promises, lyrical passages, profound parables, and endless common sense throughout the pages of the Original Text. The Bible is broad and deep, with enfolded or implicate order in meaning to almost each and every verse. If you open to a classic—the Twenty-third Psalm, for instance—and find yourself by the familiar still waters, fine. But there are also terrifying stories, genealogies (the "begats," some people call them), and seemingly tedious and detailed instructions on how to build a tabernacle or test a wife for faithfulness.

If you should open your Book to a less-than-pleasant place, do not be dismayed. There are tough times and great times in any and every life. And the Bible points them out—rough places as well as plain.

Mark the date next to the phrase or word that caught your attention. Write in your Bible if you want to do so. Keep a separate notebook if that appeals to you. This is your process of discovery.

Be honest. If you have a hostile reaction, write that down. If you think you merely like the sound of a phrase, write that down.

If you need the Bible for only a moment's comfort, don't close the Book before you make a note of the place where that comfort was found. And if you are disturbed when you read and feel unsettled, that is good news. The Bible texts can stir up our suppressed feelings and bring them into the open air and light of day to be examined and dealt with—if not today, soon.

Be wise. Make notes of your own observations. Cherish them. But don't necessarily share your first discoveries with friends, family, or temple or church. The process of reading the Bible is about you—where you are and where you are going. Like your own life, the Bible relates to itself. Patterns appear and develop as you look at more than one part or one moment of your life. Patterns appear in the Bible as you look at more than one line, one phrase.

Necessary Tool

You don't need a degree in theology to appreciate what the Bible is saying. But you do need a Bible concordance. A concordance is an alphabetical index to biblical words with a reference to the sentence in which each word appears and usually some part of the context. Concordances are also available on CD, and online at no cost via the Internet. Strong's Exhaustive Concordance of the Bible—the easiest to use and most thorough concordance to the King James Version of the Bible—shows every word of that translation of the Bible in alphabetical order. Each word is assigned a number for cross-reference to the original Hebrew or Greek word. Strong's numbering system is used by most other biblical references that use the original Hebrew or Greek. Many versions of the Bible contain concordances as well as maps, alternate readings, dictionaries, chain references, and textual footnotes. Some Bibles used by Christians contain the words of Jesus in red print. The Strong's Concordance used to write this book is found at www.crosswalk.com, which has nearly thirty Bible translations online in one place and concordances available at a click.

Wikipedia.com explains:

Strong's Exhaustive Concordance of the Bible is a concordance of the King James Bible (KJV) that was constructed under the direction of Dr. James Strong (1822–1894). Dr. Strong was professor of exegetical theology at Drew Theological Seminary at the time. It is an exhaustive cross-reference of every word in the KJV back to the word in the Original Text. It included:

- The 8674 Hebrew root words used in the Old Testament. (Example: Hebrew word #570 in Strong's—'emesh)
- The 5523 Greek root words used in the New Testament. (Example: Greek word #3056 in Strong's—Logos)

Using a concordance not only tells you where to find words in the Bible but can totally transform your understanding of the Book. As the Bible often speaks in allegory, simile, and parable, a concordance easily takes you into those dimensions of thought.

Take, for example, the word *Lebanon*. Most know it as a once-peaceful, later war-torn country bordering Israel and Syria—a country still war-torn and in difficult, difficult circumstances. Strong's Concordance shows that the word *Lebanon* appears seventy-one times in the King James Version and assigns Lebanon the number 3844. Turning to number 3844 in Strong's, you will see that the word *Lebanon* is from the Hebrew root for *heart* (the most interior organ) and defines *Lebanon* as "white mountain" (from its snow top). Some of the biblical references to Lebanon may be merely geographical. But others connote much more.

"Is it not yet a very little while, and Lebanon shall be turned into a fruitful field, and the fruitful field shall be esteemed as a forest?" (Isaiah 29:17).

If the word *Lebanon* here is read as meaning "your heart," the verse takes on a new, richer meaning. Read it again and substitute "my heart" for "Lebanon."

"Is it not yet a very little while, and my heart shall be turned into a fruitful field. . . ."

Any word in the Bible can be looked up in the same way. Should you want to know how to be a better mother, how to get along with your own mother, or what being a mother might mean to your spiritual as well as biological life, then you will want to fulfill that desire and start by looking up the word *mother* in your Bible concordance. You will find nearly three hundred references to "mother"—the first in Genesis 2:24.

But to find the Mother who is the Spirit of God, one needs to look up the words for God or Lord used in both the Hebrew and King James or other translations. The translations have substituted the word *God* or *Lord* whereas in the Original Text, as we shall see in this book in subsequent chapters, God is often described with a feminine-gender word or words. In many places in Genesis the original Hebrew name for God is "The Breasted One." Both the King James Version and the Hebrew Bible translations use, instead, Lord or God, or Lord God. Throughout the pages of this book you will see numerous places in the Bible where the original female nature of God has been glossed over or simply mistranslated.

The Pesky Begats

Even the "begats" can take on new meaning if we use a concordance. The first genealogy listed in the Bible is in the fifth chapter of Genesis—the genealogy of Adam, Seth, Enos, Cainan, Mahaleel, Jared, Enoch, Methuselah, Lamech, Noah. This genealogy can make your eyes glaze over. If you read the list literally, skim over it, or dismiss it as an example demonstrating that the Bible is about men long dead, you will miss the message. But with a little digging into your concordance, what on the surface looks like a boring chronological history of generations becomes, instead, a spiritual message reframing the names in the list.

A translation in one interpretation of the Hebrew meaning (and there is often more than one meaning to a Hebrew or any word) suggests Man (*Adam*), Places (*Seth*), Incurable Sickness (*Enos*), Deplorable (*Cainan*), The Blessed God (*Mahaleel*), Descends

(*Jared*), Teaching (*Enoch*), Death Sent Away (*Methuselah*), to the Distressed (*Lamech*), Comfort/Rest (*Noah*). Read as narrative, the list of names says that man placed in incurable sickness is deplorable, and therefore the Blessed God descends, teaching that death be sent away and bringing to the distressed comfort and rest.

This may seem a stretch at first glance. But it seems less so if you are familiar with a concordance, those names in Hebrew, the variety of their implications and interpretations, and the fact that the Bible's message is not about patriarchy but about the nondenominational Spirit of God: the Creative Mother caring for her children—for you.

Millions upon hundreds of millions today turn to the Bible. Some do so in an irksome self-righteousness, others from terror, others more for hope, for guidance through the complexities of the world. You have turned in quiet to the Bible for some glimpses of what it might hold for you. You have chosen a Bible that suits you, reached into a verse or text, an easy or hard place, listened, watched, made a note, kept it to yourself.

Now, how to begin a fuller journey into the pages of the Bible and your spiritual life? Without anyone looking over your shoulder, to catch sight of the Bible as a whole, to find the female Principle of God, turn to the beginning and the opening words of the Book: *In the beginning God created the heaven and the earth* (Genesis 1:1).

Our journey is under way.

Notes

1. *Whose Bible Is It? A Short History of the Scriptures* by Jaroslav Pelikan (Penguin, 2005) is the best and easiest book to read on the history of the Bible and its translations and compilations.

2. *God's Secretaries: The Making of the King James Bible* by Adam Nicolson (Perennial, 2004) is an exhaustive, entertaining, illustrated account of the translators and translation of the King James Bible.

1

In the Beginning

In the beginning God created the heaven and the earth.
—Genesis 1:1

What if the biblical God is not male?

What if the biblical Creator, in the original language of the Bible, is spoken of as a female Spirit?

Genesis 1:1 to 2:3 describes the Creation of the universe by an all-good, all-powerful God. The Creation—not just of all objects, but also of all ideas—sets the tone for the entire Bible. All else, all the remainder of the pages that make up the texts of the Hebrew and Christian holy words are commentaries. Backgrounds and foregrounds, highlights and dim places, all politics, history, art, relations between men and women, all stand in relation to the first chapter of Genesis.

Let's look at what the opening lines of the Bible say about the Creator:

> In the beginning God created the heaven and the earth.
>
> And the earth was without form, and void; and darkness was upon the face of the deep. And the Spirit of God moved upon the face of the waters. (Genesis 1:1–2)

Spirit of God, in the original Hebrew, is *ruah Elohim. Ruah,* the word meaning "Spirit," is a feminine noun. *Elohim* is a grammatical feminine plural form of God. Nothing is said about a bearded old man in flowing white robes. What is said is that Spirit, denoted

11

by a feminine word and a feminine plural word, is Creator and moves.

As we read the Bible, we should not forget that all life springs from Spirit. There is no fearsome Father to run from, no overbearing Mother, no absent Parent to search for. Remind yourself; make a note if you need to: no matter what you might have heard before, the Creator is not a large man. This reminder will help clarify the Bible for you. The God of the Bible is described as feminine Spirit.

Repeated Themes

The ideas outlined in the early verses of Genesis may seem simple to you, or they may take some time to absorb. What the Bible says in its first verses may seem either literal or abstract, so that you may just want to skim the surface and turn to stories of women and men found later in the Bible and this book. But even if you don't begin at the beginning, you will want to return to the ideas expressed in the early biblical verses, because the deeper meanings of biblical stories are found there.

As we shall see in the first chapter of Genesis and throughout the Bible, the concern of the Creator, Spirit, is not only Creation but also conception, comfort, providence, wisdom, and immortal life. The Bible is a timeless, self-referential text; there is hardly a line, book, or story that does not relate to another in its pages. Themes repeat themselves, as do significant words and ideas. To start with the misconception that God is exclusively a male and not, as the text says, a feminine-plural creative force, is to read through the pages of Scripture not in the light of the text but under a shadow.

You will want to read this Creation account for yourself. For now, let's slip under the face of biblical waters, look into the well of Scripture and its overarching themes, and see just a glimpse of the bounty that lies beneath the surface of a few key words in the first chapter of the Bible.

Two Kinds of Time

If you have ever dipped into biblical waters, you will have already recognized that in the Bible things happen in two different kinds of time. The opening words in the Bible describe one kind of time. "In the beginning" time is spiritual, synchronous, simultaneous coexistence—everything good that ever was or will be happening in a present moment. We hint at this kind of time when we speak of immortality or eternal life, when we say "forever."

Simultaneous time can't be measured or budgeted by a clock or the lowering and rising of sun or tides. It's not variable. The message of synchronous times is spiritual, perfect, and unvarying—not "I loved you on July 31, but not on August 9." The first chapter of Genesis describes only simultaneous time.

The second chapter of Genesis introduces time as measurable in hours, days, and years, time that can be measured by the clock and by genealogies. It is historical and chronological—the "my mother was born in . . ." or "I'll meet you at eight o'clock" kind of time.

The distinction is important. Among other things, the distinction explains miracles. What we call miracles happen at the intersection of the two kinds of time—timeless truth meeting the lives of men and women and nations in clock time.

The time referred to as "in the beginning" describes Spirit—God extending, appearing, and acting throughout the cosmos simultaneously. This kind of time is freedom, endless bliss, perfect peace, continuing spiritual and scientific exploration. This kind of time can reach you wherever you are in chronological or clock time, and these two kinds of time intersect throughout the Bible pages.

Water

Water plays such an important role in the Bible that one cannot possibly consider only its literal meaning. As we have read in Genesis 1:2, the Spirit of God moves on the face of the waters. In major events of early chapters of the Bible to come—the Ark and the Flood, the parting of the Red Sea—water is also a metaphor for the physical manifestation of the first named element of Creation. There is a lifetime of study of biblical water—seas, oceans, rivers, rain, snow, hail, dew, and the mixture of water and light, the rainbow.

The Voice, Light, First Day

The revelation of Creation comes into focus with the words, "And God said." The first thing God said is, "Let there be light" (Genesis 1:3).

In Genesis the original Hebrew word for "light" is *or*—often referred to or translated as "revelation" or "truth" (or both). Light, like water, streams throughout the Bible. When we say that we "see the light" on a topic or idea, we are referring to seeing the truth of something.

All Creation in the first chapter of Genesis takes place in the light. Though there is yet no sun, moon, or stars, still there is light. Creation is revealed; more specifically, the truth of what already exists is revealed.

An example is, when you're moving through a darkened house, things can be felt though nothing can be seen. At hand is a light switch. Touch it and the room floods with light. In stages, the eye takes in every inch, every nook and cranny, everything that has been purposefully, carefully, artfully placed in a room for nourishment, comfort, and rest.

In a way, that is how Genesis 1:3 introduces the nuances of Creation. Everything is there, but the light makes it visible.

And God saw the light, that it was good: and God divided the light from the darkness.

And God called the light Day and the darkness he called Night. And the evening and the morning were the first day. (Genesis 1:4–5)

For the first day of Creation—the division of light from darkness—the word *first* is used; the following days are designated second through seventh. The unity and oneness of Creation by *Elohim* is further clarified in that choice of the cardinal ordinance—*a first day*.

God's words define and make distinctions. There is one Source, but not one big blur. So, in the first verses of Genesis, light is day and not night. And as we read on we see what we now take for granted: morning is not evening, the dry land is not water, fruit trees are not grass, the moon is not the sun, birds are not whales. Each and every idea is distinct and individual and moves in the context of the *ruah Elohim*—Spirit of God.

Revelation, the last book of the Bible, graphically depicts light and darkness. Try tracking the word *light* all the way to the end of the Bible to see a glimpse of the spiritual signification described in this first chapter of the Book.

The Second Day

And God said, Let there be a firmament in the midst of the waters, and let it divide the waters from the waters.

And God made the firmament, and divided the waters which were under the firmament from the waters which were above the firmament: and it was so.

And God called the firmament Heaven. And the evening and the morning were the second day. (Genesis 1:6–8)

After the Light of the first day and the visibility that comes with the Light, there is the second day spoken into being by the Voice that clarifies—that brings understanding through a division of one thing from another. And it is all harmony or Heaven though there is still no earth.

The Third Day

By the third day Creation is pregnant with activity and implicate, enfolded order (Genesis 1:9–13). References to the "third day" appear throughout the Bible and indicate a change between the historical story-in-time and the spiritual present in-the-beginning time. As you stay alert to the *third day* in biblical texts, you will see that when that day is mentioned the story moves into another dimension.

In this original third day, dry land appears and the seas are gathered. This same *ruah Elohim* says:

> "Let the earth sprout vegetation: seed-bearing plants and
> fruit trees of every kind on earth that bear fruit with the seed
> in it." And it was so. The earth brought forth vegetation,
> seed-bearing plants of every kind, and trees of every kind
> bearing fruit with the seed in it. And God saw that this was
> good. And there was evening and morning, a third day.
> (Genesis: 1:11–13 TNK)

The text indicates that every plant, every tree, every thing and idea already exists.

The seed is within itself, says the King James Version. Every plant and tree, every thing and every idea are already made, not in an hour or a year but in in-the-beginning time where everything already made is made.

Attacks on the Seed

At this point in Genesis there is no creation of—nor division of— male and female. Later, after gender and sex are introduced into biblical accounts, attacks are made on the seed of the woman. The question will be asked: Are these attacks on woman or attacks on the Spirit of God and Creation? As we trace the word *seed* and the lives of the women in Scripture through the Bible, the answer becomes clear: the woman is the surrogate for the attack on the Creation of *ruah Elohim*. Woman is the scapegoat, not merely for men or society, but for attacks on the Creation revealed in the first chapter of Genesis.

The Word *Fourth*

Like *ruah* (Spirit), *fourth* is a word indicating the feminine in Hebrew. The Voice says, "Let there be two great lights" (Genesis 1:14). These lights divide the day from the night, as the "firmament" of verse 6 divides "the waters from the waters." The lights are "set in the firmament of heaven to give light upon the earth and to rule over the day and over the night, and to divide the light from the darkness." The light has already been divided on the second day. If these two great lights are to mean the sun and the moon, their emergence takes place in a feminine context. The lights appear for "signs and seasons" as well as for days and years. Further, the two lights are to rule over "the day and night," and the Hebrew word for "rule over" is also a feminine gender word—*Memshalah*—indicating the rule of God. And the stars also appear, as they will throughout the Bible, as a sign of fertility and birth. Everything is in its place, and it is all good.

Abundant Provision

The Voice rings out again: "Let the waters bring forth abundantly the moving creature that hath life, and fowl that may fly above the earth in the open firmament of heaven" (Genesis 1:20).

So it is too with the whales and other living creatures. The waters bring them forth "abundantly," and of the revelation of this fifth day—like the revelation of the third and fourth—it says that God saw that it was all good (Genesis 1:12, 18, 21). The use of the word *abundantly* as a reference to the first chapter of Genesis takes on added significance as the Bible texts unfold. One example is "I will abundantly bless her provision" (Psalm 132:15).

In the Bible no virtue is necessarily gained nor points awarded for starvation, physical or emotional. The biblical Creator, the Spirit of the first chapter of Genesis, provides abundantly.

Female Image

In this ascendant order of Creation, from light to day and night, to heaven and earth to seas and land to plant to fish to fowl to beast, to the sixth day and male and female, the female is the last.

> And God said, Let us make man in our image, after our likeness. . . .
>   So God created man in his own image.
> (Genesis 1:26–27)

The feminine-plural *ruah Elohim* says, in Robert Alter's Hebrew translation of Genesis, "Let us make a human in our image, by our likeness, to hold sway over the fish of the sea and the fowl of the heavens and the cattle and the wild beasts and all the crawling things that crawl upon the earth."

Alter adds in a note: "The term *'adam* (a human) is a generic term for human beings, not a proper noun (suggesting a person's name). It does not automatically suggest maleness . . . and so the traditional rendering 'man' is misleading, and an exclusively male *'adam* would make nonsense of the last clause of verse 27."

The Creation outlined in Genesis 1 is completed in the repetition by God of all the abundance that has been revealed through the words of the text. Whether one reads male and female to mean two separate genders or one image, including both genders as a compound idea, the female is the highest idea in the revelation of Spirit's unfolding Creation.

Blessed Rest

And then the crowning achievement, a seventh or Sabbath day of rest in which to survey, set a stamp on, and reflect on the whole of Creation. Just as the living creatures of the fifth day and the male and female of the sixth day are blessed, so too is this rest on the seventh day blessed (Genesis 2:3).

There are countless examples of good and blessing throughout the Bible, but when examples such as "water," "the third day," and "the seed within itself" appear in the text, they are reminders that the story is not merely historical or geographically located but points to spiritual territory. To explore and settle into spiritual territory, there are biblical texts that describe the light and the path to the place where the light dwells. But on that path the text goes to Eden, where gullible, victimized, incomplete women and weak, frightened, jealous men pass the days of their lives, young and restless, old and forlorn. One wonders why anyone could want Adam and Eve in the family tree.

Popular perception has assumed that a male God is the center of the Creation account in the first chapter of Genesis. But Creator is Spirit, a feminine-gendered word. This feminine word is overturned in chapter 2 of Genesis when another Creation account is introduced and life gets complicated under a male-gendered word for God.

2

The Seed and the Serpent

And the Lord God caused a deep sleep to fall upon Adam, and
he slept: and he took one of his ribs, and closed up the flesh
instead thereof.

—Genesis 2:21

Where is the *ruah Elohim*, the Spirit of God, in the story of
Adam and Eve? Not in the Garden of Eden, not in the Light, and
not in the biblical text. The *Spirit of God* is no longer the name for
God in chapter 2 of Genesis. Another God with another name
takes the stage.

If you are a woman, if you have ever felt that you do not have
your own distinct identity, or that you exist only in relation to a
man, or that you are walking around in a dream, blamed for things
not your fault, then you are in the land of Eve, the second account
of creation in Genesis, chapter 2.

After the first account of Creation has been spelled out, the
Bible presents a second creation—in complete contradistinction to
the first, and introducing evil.

From then on, side by side, lie the unhappy parts of the Bible—
the parts in which innocents are slaughtered and cities laid waste—
and the happy parts, in which lives are long and full and cities and
nations built up. Sometimes the two accounts of Creation are
mixed together within a sentence, verse, or story. Recognition of
these places may not come in any given moment. But the first
glimpse of a text that carries more than one message can be breathtaking.

Through the Mist

The story of Adam and Even in the Garden of Eden is not the story of spiritual Creation. The story of Adam and Eve is not really even a continuation of the first account, but a second and entirely different turned-upside-down story set against the backdrop of that revelation, in which the Spirit (female) of *Elohim* (plural, God) is visible in a light-filled, spiritual and complete universe. In fact, the story of creation in the garden is nothing compared to the first account of Creation.

Our introduction to the Garden of Eden (Genesis 2:4–3:24) goes like this: Instead of Spirit or *ruah Elohim* moving on the waters and the Word introducing Light, a mist comes up from the earth and covers everything. A new name for God appears—YHWH—and an entirely different method of creating.

It is in this second chapter of Genesis that the ills for women begin. It is this second chapter that has created, not male and female simultaneously complete, but a false notion that the genders are separate and one gender is subservient to the other. How did this happen—this idea of female subservience to the male?

Word Change

In the second chapter of Genesis, the English language uses *Lord God* to indicate YHWH or *hwhy*, from a Hebrew root word *hyh* joined to *Elohim*. Strong's Concordance to the Bible gives several definitions of that root word—among them, "to happen, to come to pass, to become like." Richard Elliott Friedman, author of *Who Wrote the Bible?* points out that only in the second and third chapters of Genesis is the appellation YHWH used. Friedman attributes that quirk to the attempt of an editor—Redactor—to soften the transition from the first to the second account of creation. Another school of thought states that they are actually two different accounts with two different names for God and two different orders of creation. The only constant in the differing accounts is that woman is created last. But in this second account she is not created good.

Another God, Another Woman

The variety of interpretations of Hebrew words and the various biblical translations leave the consequences of the second account of creation and subsequent male and female relationships to the dominant culture of a period of time. Joining the Creation by *ruah Elohim* in Genesis 1 to the reverse creation by YHWH in Genesis 2 is one way to deprive both male and female of their inherent mutual spiritual birthright. The idea that God had to re-create or add to Creation produces not only rather convoluted theology but also a second class of citizens. There is little question that no other texts have affected women in the Bible-reading world as much as those found in the opening chapters of the second chapter of Genesis. But the second creation account is in conflict with the first Creation.

Conflicting Creations

Here is how the stories conflict. The creation sketched by Genesis 2 posits that instead of Spirit moving on the face of the waters and the Word calling Light, a mist comes up from the earth and covers everything—waters the whole face of the ground. Instead of a blessed male and female emerging as the penultimate issue of *ruah Elohim*, a God with a different name makes the first man out of the dust of the ground and breathes life into him through his nose. The "dust-man" is put in a garden called Eden. The root of this word *Eden* is "pleasure." A woman is made out of the rib of the dust-man while he is sleeping. She wakes up next to a man she does not know. Poor woman. Poor Eve.

Before long she has doomed all humanity—to this day. That is what a literal, out-of-context reading of the Adam and Eve story might lead you to believe, if it stood alone. But it doesn't. Eve's story stands in contrast to the spiritual Creation in the first chapter of Genesis.

Take a fresh look at this classic tale.

Good and Not Good

Those familiar with the second chapter of Genesis will recall that some trees are put in the garden. One, in the midst of the garden, is the tree of life. The other tree, in no specific location, is a tree of the *knowledge of both good and evil*. That which is ambiguous has no life, has no place and no specificity of location.

In the description of the Garden, one river comes forth and separates into four rivers. We will see that *river* and *rivers* have special biblical signification for women; this will run through the Bible all the way to Revelation.

And Lord God tells the man to eat from any tree but the tree of the knowledge of good and evil. The warning is that if the man eats of the knowledge of good and evil, he shall surely die. Knowing evil and good together causes death. The injunction is clear: to know only good or to not know evil. Previously, in the first chapter of Genesis, good has been announced as male and female created simultaneously, not one at a time. This creation of Adam alone is already not good. In a further reversal of the Creation of Genesis 1 by *ruah Elhoim*, when this Lord God, YHWH, makes beasts and fowls, the man, instead of God, names them. But still, for Adam, there is no helper—in Hebrew, no *'ezer kenegdo*.

There are endless interpretations of and arguments over the meanings of those Hebrew words *'ezer kenegdo*. One approach suggests *ezer* may derive from the root *gre* (to be strong), not *zr* (to help), and thus the translation would read "a power equal to him." There is a multitude of opinions as to the meaning of *kenegdo*, including scholars arguing for (1) a subordination of either the man to the woman or the woman to the man, (2) equality between them, or (3) the notion of a relationship filled with tension. Translations make a difference in meaning. In the case of the Bible, with the claim of authority from God, a translation can change the entire meaning of the text.

Male and Female Translators

As the King James Version of the Bible influenced subsequent thought and language, so too, for centuries, a Hellenized Jew—Philo of Alexandria (20 B.C.E to 50 C.E.)—became the source for Jewish and Christian writers who viewed man as the head of the woman. Augustine, Aquinas, Maimonides, and Martin Luther, John Milton in his epic *Paradise Lost*, and John Knox carry themes from Philo through to the Danvers Statement of 1987, in which the Christian evangelical Council on Biblical Manhood and Womanhood said, among other things, that "Adam's headship in marriage was established by God before the Fall." Using selected biblical text, the Council included in its mission the notion that some roles in the church are restricted to men and that women should not resist their husbands' authority. The Danvers Statement, unlike the statements of earlier male writers acting alone, was drafted by both men and women.

Though the hierarchical model of biblical creation has been the majority view, occasionally—and increasingly, over time—voices have been raised, sermons preached, and articles and books written presenting a parallel view that sees both Creation accounts as propounding gender egalitarianism. For some, a modern feminist reading is introduced in the Bible's New Testament, with particular women named as apostle or deacon or the head of a church. Others point to the earlier actions of the wives of the patriarchs of Genesis to illustrate egalitarianism and female as head over the male.

Egalitarian interpretation of the first and second chapters of Genesis blossomed in the Society of Friends, particularly through the life and writings of Englishwoman Margaret Fell, who was imprisoned several times and whose seven daughters became Quaker preachers. But it is in the United States that egalitarian readings of the Genesis accounts of Creation became even more widely known and disseminated. Angelina and Sarah Grimke, converts to Quakerism, were abolitionists who asked, "What then can woman do for the slave when she is herself under the feet of man and shamed in silence?" The sisters exchanged and published letters, and Sarah's 1837 text, *The Original Equality of Woman*, was a ground-breaking exegesis on the creation accounts in Genesis.

The Shakers, founded by Ann Lee (1736–1784), note the plural nature of the word *Elohim* and consider God as both Mother and Father—a reading that we now know accords with the original text—although their interpretation of the concept of lust as the original sin led the movement to adopt celibacy. "But no one more thoroughly established the priority of the first creation account, with its intimations of gender equality, than Mary Baker Eddy," say the editors of the exhaustive and authoritative *Eve and Adam: Jewish, Christian, and Muslim Readings on Genesis and Gender* (1999). It was Mary Baker Eddy, in her 1875 edition of *Science and Health with Key to the Scriptures*, who stated, "There could be no second creation after all was made that was made, nor ever a man formed since the full idea of God was given."

In the last (1910) edition of *Science and Health*, in the chapter titled "Genesis," Mary Baker Eddy states: "It may be worthwhile here to remark that, according to the best scholars, there are clear evidences of two distinct documents in the early parts of Genesis. One is called the Elohistic, because the Supreme Being therein is called Elohim. The other document is called the Jehovistic, because Deity therein is always called Jehovah—or Lord God, as our common version translates it."

A Woman's Translation

Elizabeth Cady Stanton organized a group of women and published *The Woman's Bible* in the last decade of the 1880s. It's worth printing here a few of her words from the Appendix of that Bible

(available online at http://www.sacred-texts.com/wmn/wb/wb41
.htm). Stanton writes, "As the Revising Committee refer to a
woman's translation of the Bible as their ultimate authority, for the
Greek, Latin and Hebrew text, a brief notice of this distinguished
scholar is important: Julia Smith's translation of the Bible stands out
unique among all translations. It is the only one ever made by a
woman, and the only one, it appears, ever made by man or woman
without help."

Current Critical Exegesis

Almost one hundred years later, in 1973, Phyllis Trible offered a
paper at Andover Newton Theological Seminary that has changed
biblical scholarship and readings of the second and third chapters
of Genesis. Trible says about Eden, "The woman is both the the-
ologian and the translator." And by contrast, "The man is not dominant; he is not aggressive: he is not a decision-maker." The fact
remains that the original texts have been examined and yield a picture of God that does not remain in the hands of exclusively male
translators, and that women may continue to read the texts for
themselves and compare and contrast them to their own lives to see
to what extent the text and interpretations of them have an influence on their personal experiences, their mental and physical
health.

In the Garden

Continuing for now in Eden, in Genesis 3:1 a narrative device
occurs that is repeated again and again in the Bible. The story
that starts with a man moves to a woman and her situation or
condition—to where the action is going to take place.

A talking serpent appears out of nowhere and asks the woman,
"Did God really say, 'You must not eat from any tree in the garden?'" (NIV).

An element of doubt has been introduced. The talking serpent trivializes this, telling the woman she is wrong, that she has been sold a bill of goods. "Tush, ye shall not die" (Genesis 3:4 Tyndale), the serpent says—as if to say, never mind, it's nothing, no big deal. All the woman has to do—it's suggested—is to eat fruit that looks good and makes one wise, and then she will be like God (or gods, depending on the translation) and know good and evil. Trivialized and seduced to death, the woman eats. She gives some to her husband. He eats.

Things do change, but not, in this case, for the better. The woman is ashamed, not wise, although she *is* searching for wisdom. The entire Bible is replete with references to female wisdom and wise women and references to God as Wisdom. The Book of Proverbs is one example, in which women are designated wise, particularly in verses 1:20–21, 3:5–5, 7:4–5, 9:8–9, 14:1, and 31:10–31. The woman in Eden is not wise, but she is to be ashamed—perhaps the consequence of holding two conflicting ideas in conscious thought at the same time. "Adam . . . where art thou?" asks the Lord God. Adam says that he was hiding from God. Lord God asks if Adam has eaten the fruit—a mere question.

It's Her Fault

The man answers, "The woman thou gavest to be with me, she gave me of the tree and I did eat" (Genesis 3:12). Whereas the man points the responsibility to Lord God, then to the woman, and last to himself, the woman sticks to reporting the facts. "What is this you have done?" Lord God asks the woman. She answers directly: "The serpent deceived me, and I ate" (Genesis 3:13 NIV). Lord God curses the serpent and puts hatred between the serpent and the woman and between the seed of the serpent and the seed of the woman—introducing a theme that appears throughout the Bible. The culmination of this hatred is found in Revelation 12, in which this clash in Eden is writ large—the woman is now clothed with the sun and the moon under her feet of the feminine fourth day of *ruah Elohim's* Creation, and the serpent has now grown into a great red dragon.

Bodily Consequences

The struggle of women and their offspring, attacked and then saved from hatred, threads throughout the Scriptures. The Book of Psalms, Isaiah, Jeremiah, Micah, John, 1 Thessalonians, and Revelation speak of the woman in travail. The woman in Eden, named Eve, is to have sorrow in childbirth, but even that chimerical account does not say that is to be the case for her descendants. Much territory remains to be explored on the subject of how Eve affects women's bodies today. There is no question that women's bodies have become a battlefield for a host of opinions and ills.

Many generations of women have referred to the monthly menstrual cycle as "the curse," and as language has such power, this curse on Eve has filtered into consciousness through time. Investigations into different standards of medical treatment for women and men reflect layers and layers of Adam-like assumptions. The recent past assumption has been that, with the exception of sexual organs, women and men's bodies are the same. Assuming a male body to be the standard for all bodies has resulted in research that drew conclusions based solely on male subjects, with repercussions in every area of women's health. There is, however, a correlation between revised views of the creation of Genesis, chapter 2, and an increase in attention to women's health and singular nature. The chasm of negative consequences that result from the Eve story are only now being probed, but as new scholarship and reading show Eve absolved of guilt, women pay more attention to their own health care and the standards improve.

Another verse has left a legacy. "And unto the man he said, 'Because you have listened to the voice of your wife, and have eaten of the tree about which I commanded you, "You shall not eat of it," cursed is the ground because of you; in toil you shall eat of it all the days of your life'" (Genesis 3:17 NRSV). Men who find it painful to listen to women's voices or instructions may be hanging onto the notion that they, like Adam, are cursed because they listened to their wives. But one conclusion is inescapable: accepting the guilt of Adam is hard work and not profitable. In sharp contrast to this condemnation of Adam for listening to the voice of Eve, the biblical men who do listen to women and whom we find in succeeding pages, are the ones we remember today. Abraham, Isaac, Jacob, David, Jesus, and Paul listen to women and act on what women say to them.

What You Think About Creation

Let's reflect on the creation accounts so far. Separating one account from another is essential to making sense of biblical stories and messages.

Dismissing the narrative of Adam and Eve as "merely" myth is difficult for many reasons. It is impossible to dismiss any part of the Bible if you believe that the Book is the inspired Word of God. So much of life seems equally as convoluted as the drama in the garden that even though we may not believe that man is literally made out of dust nor woman from a rib, the roots of this myth run very deep.

Inconsistencies between the two creations abound. The account of the Garden of Eden occurs in a mist, not Light. We now see the contrast between the account of Creation by *ruah Elohim* and an account of creation by a hypothetical, mythological God that suggests that the consequence of doubt and ambiguity is suffering. But this does not mean the Bible tells us about two real gods.

The Bible indicates that what people think about God—how they apprehend the Supreme Being—determines and directs their experience. The Bible also describes how people understand and follow God in different ways. And, most of all, the Bible tracks how God becomes *all* to human thought and flesh.

Until that day, you may find in the story of Eve the message that a woman without her own distinct spiritual identity or consciousness is going to be in trouble.

Begats Have Meaning

"This is the book of the generations of Adam. In the day that God created man, in the likeness of God made he him; Male and Female created he them; and blessed them, and called their name Adam, in the day when they were created" (Genesis 5:1–2).

Here in the biblical text is the man, the male and female of Genesis 1:27 and Adam from Genesis 2:7–22, mixed together in the language of the translators of the King James Bible, presented as the original word and not a narrator's mingling of texts.

What follows in Genesis 5:6–32 is a genealogy that can be read as an impossible list of male *begats* or as an encoded message of hope. As mentioned earlier, one translation of the Hebrew words reads: Man (Adam), Placed (Seth), Incurable Sickness (Enos), Deplorable (Cainan), The Blessed God (Mahaheel), Descends (Jared), Teaching (Enoch), Death Sent Away (Methusaleh), to the Distressed (Lamech), Comfort/Rest (Noah).

The Flood

Even the most inexperienced Bible reader has heard about Noah, the Ark, and the Flood. The Flood comes as if to wipe away the Adam and Eve story and its repercussions. Humankind can start fresh, without the burden of the First Couple. God—The Existing One is one translation—establishes a covenant, a promise, and a contract with Noah.

Included in the story of Noah, in the midst of the Flood, are more glimpses of the first vision of Creation: God gives Noah seven days' warning; the animals are brought into the ark both male and female; and the ark is lifted above the earth on the waters—the waters upon which the Spirit of God, *ruah Elohim* moved in turn moves the ark and its inhabitants.

The ark represents safety and security, a place evil or danger cannot reach. "And God remembered Noah, and every living thing" (Genesis 8:1). There is reason to consider that the biblical male and female to come in the chapters that follow are the descendants, not of Adam and Eve, but of the family of Noah, who made a safe voyage into the elements of the spiritual Creation. Adam and Eve are dead. What reason could there possibly be to hold on to their curse?

3

The Breasted One

And Sarah said, God hath made me to laugh, so that all that hear will laugh with me.

—Genesis 21:6

What kind of a God tells husbands to obey their wives?

The God of the Bible, the God of Creation, says to Abraham, "In all that Sarah hath said unto thee, hearken unto her voice" (Genesis 21:12).

The story of Abraham and Sarah and Hagar has been read for centuries as a patriarchal text. Now, through new scholarship, revelation, and common sense, it is clear that the God of these texts is not a fearsome male God but a Mothering God. It is also obvious that the texts relate a narrative of spiritual power coming to women, woman as agent for change, the rights of women acknowledged. And both genders, without regard to nationality, hear and speak to God. Hagar and Abraham both have births foretold, both have children who receive a blessing.

Ruah Elohim, the Creator of the first chapter of Genesis, appears with new names in the lives of the first matriarch, her maid, and her husband, who all become real to us through these appearances. As *ruah Elohim* enters their lives, biblical women and men are no longer myths or abstract concepts, but appear as real people with whom we can identify. And the Spirit of God has intense concerns involving compassion, fertility, life, and identity.

A closer reading of the lives and texts from Genesis 11 on through the story of Abraham, Sarah, and Hagar has revised what we once thought about God's nature and names and what the Bible is saying about women. In these texts:

- God comes to powerless women
- God controls conception
- Ticking biological clocks are rewound
- The curse in childbirth is reversed
- Children are a blessing
- A woman sees God face to face
- A woman identifies God and gives God a name
- God announces for Herself a new name
- Laughter is introduced
- A man weeps for a woman

More Than History

The story begins in Genesis 11, just a chapter and a half after the Flood, with these words of the King James Version translation:

> Now these are the generations of Terah: Terah begat Abram, Nahor, and Haran; and Haran begat Lot. (Genesis 11:27)

In one verse it looks as if the story is about some men, the generations of Terah. But the Bible often makes a statement and then leaves out the part that will later be seen as relevant for the development of the more spiritual idea. This is what happens here. In two verses of the Bible we will learn a family history that impacts the world even today.

One of the many ways in which the Bible is instructive is in its simple telling of a story. The accounts are often so sparse, perhaps ambiguous, that the reader fills in the blanks, raising questions even where there are none. The Bible becomes the background and the reader's thought the foreground, played out on the canvas of a desert landscape. And behind even the desert landscape *ruah Elohim* moves, speaks, and appears.

Haran dies, and the text moves right along, focusing ever more sharply on the main point.

> And Abram and Nahor took them wives: the name of
> Abram's wife was Sarai. . . . (Genesis 11:29)

The next verse tells what the story is actually about.

> But Sarai was barren; she had no child. (Genesis 11:30)

This is not to be merely a story about a child born to a woman and her husband. As we read it, this story speaks, rather, to the unfolding of the days of spiritual Creation in Genesis 1 and the continuing displacement of clock time with synchronous time. Another way to frame the idea of synchronous time is to say that God insists on becoming all that exists. In this story to come, the curses from Eden are lifted, clock time falls in the face of spiritual time, and Judeo-Islamic-Christian history begins in full.

Process and Cost

The story of Abram and Sarai (her name means "princess") starts a fascinating progression of biblical women who conceive despite what we know today of the patterns of biology. In fact, Sarai is an example of a breakthrough in conception, although at this point, early in the account, there is no indication that either she or Abram wanted children.

Perhaps the princess Sarai liked being a childless princess, free to travel with Abram. Perhaps he liked it that way too. Or is there a suspicion that the culture of the times demanded children? Whatever the case, as their story begins, we know only that she was married and barren.

Out of the Blue

With no previous announcement, God speaks to Abram who is called to "get up and go [*lekh lekha*]" from his father's house to a land that he will be shown. For Abram and Sarai, leaving their father's house and starting over is essential. Their move breaks family patterns, and in the process God, rather than any biological mother and father, is revealed as benevolent Parent. God will be with them throughout their lives.

The Bible: An American Translation continues their story in these easy-to-read words: "When he was on the point of entering Egypt, he said to his wife Sarai, 'See now, I know that you are such a beautiful woman that when the Egyptians see you, they will say, "This is his wife." And they will kill me in order to keep you. Please say that you are my sister, so that I may be well treated for your sake, and my life spared through you'" (Genesis 12:11–13 AT).

Current reactions to these statements of Abram are mixed. The idea that he is manipulative and dishonest and Sarai is silent property is heard most often. But the text itself actually indicates that he is asking—not telling—his wife, that he treats her as equal in this journey, that he understands possible implications for her and their marriage, and that this may be the wisest thing to do. Further, she is his half-sister, though the text will divulge that information only later.

"The Egyptians saw that the woman was very beautiful and she was taken into Pharaoh's household and Abram was well treated for her sake" (Genesis 12:14–16 AT). Abram owes Sarai his life. Although we hear nothing from Sarai, she does seem to be the pivotal figure in the couple's mutual journey. The Pharaoh, angry with Abram for tricking him, sends the couple off with cattle, silver, and gold added to the riches he had already acquired in Egypt. No mention is made that either Abram or Sarai suffer from this episode. It is as if they can do no wrong. Sarai is passed off as Abram's sister again later, but for now, the Divine Being makes a startling announcement to the childless couple:

> And I will make thy seed as the dust of the earth: so that
> if a man can number the dust of the earth, then shall thy
> seed also be numbered. (Genesis 13:16)

Seeds and Stars

In this promise are words from both the first story of Creation and the second—*seed* and *dust*: the seed within itself from the third day of Creation in the first chapter of Genesis, and dust, the stuff of which Adam was made, as recounted in the second chapter of Genesis. Here is a glimmer of reforming the Adam story—a glimmer of *Elohim* taking control over "the dust." Adam and Eve are no longer the parents. The Spirit of God is to be in charge of human conception and affirm the multiplication of ideas, as in the first Creation. This is a promise from the Creator that things will evolve, and an indication—as we shall see in the later promises to Abraham—that there are stages of consciousness involved in the fulfillment of this promise that the seed will be multiplied.

One of the stages in this evolution is a strange meeting and a communion. We read that Abram encounters the king of Salem (peace), Melchizedek, who brings him bread and wine and who blesses him and introduces still another name for God—El Elyon, or God the Most High, possessor of heaven and earth (Genesis 14:18–20). As Abram and Sarai—and we the readers—journey, new views and designations for *Elohim* reveal themselves.

This simple meal and blessing and additional name of Deity seems to have significance in the life of the couple from one experience to the next. One way to read the Bible is to stop at this point and use a Bible concordance to look up *bread* and *wine*. There is richness involved even in what seems to be the simplest progression of events. Not only are bread and wine a timeless part of human life, but their spiritual meaning indicates glimpses of the profound provision available at every stage and state of a journey and of consciousness. There is a sacred idea implicit in this encounter in the desert, for after this exchange with bread and wine

God gives yet another new description of Divinity: "I am thy shield, and thy exceeding great reward" (Genesis 15:1)—or, as the Hebrew translation says, "I am a shield to you: Your reward shall be very great" (TNK/JPS).

And after this bread and wine blessing, as Abram questions God, stuck in the idea that he is childless and that perhaps his steward will inherit all the couple's goods, the promise to him now evolves:

> "Look up to the heavens, and count the stars, if you can count them." And He said, "So shall be your seed."
> (Genesis 15:5 JPS)

Not Adam and Eve

Now Abram's seed will not be made from dust, as was Adam. Biblical thought is not a straight line narrative, but starts with one idea and moves beyond that into a broader one. For example, there is still the *third day* reference to the seed, but the relationship is now not to dust but to the *fourth day* creation of the stars and luminaries. The *fourth day* has a feminine gender, and we may be reminded by that day and gender that *Elohim* creates. No longer children of dust as in the second chapter of creation, Abram's heirs are to be numberless children of light. God's spiritual Creation is revealing itself to human thought as Abram's consciousness has moved from one phase, one day, of spiritual Creation to the next. If we are meant to learn from biblical experience, then we may learn from Abram and Sarai's experience that Spirit's promises come true, but that fulfillment does not always come with the first dawning of an idea.

There may be significance to the fact that the promised heirs are to be reminiscent of the *fourth day*. More research needs to be done on the full meaning of the *fourth day* and its relationship to people; nevertheless, it is at this point that we hear that Sarai does want a child, and to that end she makes a decision.

Consequences

Sarai says to Abram, "The Lord has kept me from having children. Go, sleep with my maidservant; perhaps I can build a family through her" (Genesis 16:2 NIV). Abram agreed to what Sarai said.

What must she have been thinking? Though Sarai's offer to send Abram to her slave girl's bed may seem selfless or even stupid, though it may seem that trouble is bound to ensue, the Bible (contrary to traditional notions that throughout its pages women are judged) passes no judgment on her actions. It simply tells the story:

> He slept with Hagar, and she conceived. When she knew
> she was pregnant, she began to despise her mistress.
> (Genesis 16:4 NIV)

As quickly as the Bible says what happens, Hagar now has the upper hand over her mistress and despises her. Sarai tells Abram she recognizes that she has made a big mistake. She feels an injustice has been done, that Abram is to blame. Sarai, like Eve, admits her mistake and recognizes now that it is God, not her husband, who can correct the mistake. Abram also recognizes that it is not up to him to resolve this situation. He tells Sarai it is up to her to figure this out. She has been and is in charge. She is responsible for her own conscious understanding of God. Sarai asks God to judge the matter directly (Genesis 16:5–6).

We may miss this profound biblical point that women are in charge of their own decisions and their own understanding of God if we read into the Bible our own limited knowledge of the history of those times. There is a widely held belief that women of Sarai's time had no legal rights or status. But the story of Sarai and Abram is not a story of women with no legal rights or status. As for polygamy, Sarai was wife to Pharaoh at Abram's suggestion that she declare herself his sister. Abram's taking a second wife is the result, in a reversal of the early arrangement, of Sarai's prompting. As one reads the Bible stories as they are written, one sees that the patriarch was not the absolute ruler of his household—father, provider, king, judge, and husband responsible for everything and everybody. The women in biblical stories make pivotal decisions, and the men obey, follow, and go along.

Hagar despises Sarai. The Bible text feels no need to analyze Hagar's emotions. Human reaction is often inexplicable, and that may well be enough for us to know. In fact, that may well be the point. However, not surprisingly, in a home where one woman despises another, there is trouble. Sarai, on the defensive, is hard on Hagar, and so Hagar, not a long-suffering slave or martyr, runs away from the abuse.

Angels and Powerless Women

For the first time in the Bible, an angel appears, and not to a man, but to a woman—a woman suffering, alone, foreign, a slave. Hagar is only the first in a long line of biblical women whose children are announced or named by angelic representatives. This woman, Hagar, is the choice of God (as the Bible often does not distinguish between God and an angel). The angel comes to Hagar beside a spring of waters—a biblical code for the presence of "Spirit moving on the face of the waters." The angel asks the questions of the ages: "where have you come from, and where are you going?" (Genesis 16:8 NIV).

Does she not know? Does she not look deeper at the hint the water gives? Hagar merely answers directly and to the point, as all women in the Bible do: "I flee from the face of my mistress Sarai" (Genesis 16:8). The angel tells her to return to Sarai and gives Hagar the same quantitative promise that has been unfolding to Abram—the promise that her descendants will be too numerous to count (Genesis 16:10–11)—and Hagar hears: "Behold, thou art with child, and shalt bear a son, and shalt call his name Ishmael; because the LORD hath heard thy affliction." Ishmael means "God has heard."

New Names

Hagar calls the name of the Lord who had addressed her "*El-roi,*" which renames the spring of water—"Well of the Living One Who Sees Me"—as she was seen by God.

Abram is now ninety-nine years old. Now God with a new name—*El Shaddai*—appears. This is the seventh time God has appeared to Abram—a reaffirmation of the seventh day of Creation, on which *Elohim* rested and saw that all that was made was very good. Most English translations and some Hebrew translations have used the word *Almighty* for Shaddai. But scholarship over the last century has brought to light that the word means "The Breasted One." As Rabbi Arthur Waskow says, "In the Bible all the blessings in which Shaddai is over and over invoked are about fruitfulness and fertility. God is seen as Infinite Mother, pouring forth blessings from the Breasts Above and the Womb below, from the heavens that pour forth nourishing rain, from the ocean deeps that birth new life" (http://www.shalomctr.org/comment/reply/303).

Abram's descendants are to be a great nation, and a covenant is to be established between God and Abram—now renamed Abraham by the Almighty, Shaddai. It is with the new names of God and of Abraham and Sarah that the story will continue or begin again.

In a sense of coming full circle, it is not merely Abraham who is renamed. Sarai becomes Sarah, which means *abundance*—as in Genesis 1:21, in which the "waters bring forth life abundantly."

Abraham can't see it yet. "To a hundred year old will a child be born, will ninety year old Sarah give birth?" He literally falls on his face laughing.

It will be all about the laughter. El Shaddai says the son to be born will be called Isaac—identical in Hebrew with *yitshaq,* or "laughed." "And, as for Ishmael, I have heard thee" (Genesis 17:20).

The sticky part of the covenant is that Abraham and all the males of his house are to be circumcised—the foreskin suggested as having some relation to the heart and stubborn pride. The Bible and God's voice tells us twice of the event and later commands, "Circumcise therefore the foreskin of your heart, and be no more stiffnecked" (Deuteronomy 10:16).

A Visitation

Now, in more than physicality Abraham is a changed man, and Sarah, in turn, is a changed woman. Their entire story so far has been told in six chapters. They have left their homeland, journeyed through Egypt and back and around, gained riches, and met kings and potentates; Hagar has conceived; God has made seven promises to Abraham; their names have been changed, their perceptions altered.

The altered dimension is indicated more fully by the next chapter in their lives. This God, El Shaddai, called The Lord or Almighty in many translations, appeared to "Abraham in the oak grove of Mamre as he sat in his tent door in the heat of the day" says Tyndale—an early English translation. The King James Version says that "he was sitting in the door of his tent by the plains of Mamre; and he sat in the tent door in the heat of the day" (Genesis 18:1).

The texts agree that all that is to happen next happens in the presence of the Almighty or El Shaddai. None of them agree on the right word to describe the surrounding geography. And there is not agreement on whether we are to think that the day is getting hot and the patriarch was looking for a cool breeze, or that the heat of the day means noon and would allude to the height of the sun from the *fourth day* of Creation, as the sun is high in the heavens, and the word *tent* can also mean house or consciousness ("I shall dwell in the house of the Lord forever" in the Twenty-third Psalm).

Although the brief description may be read as simply "Abraham is sitting in the door of his tent trying to stay out of the heat," it can also be read that he was sitting half in, half out of his body and thoughts of the El Shaddai. It's not an uncommon experience to be so caught up in meditation or prayer that one forgets one's body for a time—a thousand years ago, the great scholar and physician Maimonides suggested that Abraham was having a vision. It is in this state that Abraham lifts up his eyes (a biblical signal the story is going to move into another more spiritual dimension) and sees three men come to visit, unexpectedly and uninvited. Abraham leaps up and bows himself to the ground. He acts the host. He begs the men to stay, washes their feet, bids them rest under a tree, and fetches bread to comfort their hearts.

Conception

Abraham's relationship with Sarah takes a turn. He doesn't ask or consult with her, but runs to her and tells her to get three measures of meal and bake cakes; then, in a rush, runs to the herd for a calf for meat; takes butter, milk, and the calf that has been cooked and sets it all before the men, then stands beside them as they eat under the tree. Each of the items that Abraham prepares has a spiritual signification, all elaborated on in later biblical texts, just as Sarah's three measures of meal find reference in Matthew and Luke.

The first thing the men say is, "Where is Sarah, thy wife?" (Genesis 18:9).

No discussion of the weather or politics or the economy. Biblical people do not engage in meandering conversations. They get right to the point.

Abraham says that Sarah is in the tent, in contrast to his being in the doorway of the tent. The men repeat what El Shaddai—The Breasted One—has already told Abraham: there will be a child next year. But this time Sarah has overheard the announcement, and although the King James Version has Sarah saying, "After I am waxed old shall I have pleasure, my lord being old also?" (Genesis 18:12), the translation is a rather sedate and coy version of what is meant, as in Hebrew there is a sense that the word translated as *pleasure* may mean moisture or lust.

Sarah laughs at the news. It is all about the laughter in the conception of their child. She denies that she laughed. In proof that one cannot hide from Spirit, The Breasted One responds, "Nay; but thou didst laugh" (Genesis 18:15). Sarah is not punished nor chided for her denial. God, with whom women converse easily and who converses easily with them, knows everything.

The story moves from laughter and conception to righteousness and destruction—toward Sodom and Gomorrah and Abraham's very intimate and challenging dialogue with God. Abraham negotiates with God to save the people in the cities. He has gained in stature and confidence and is so friendly with his God that he can argue with Her easily.

Line of Women

Again, the Bible is interested not merely in chronological time but also in synchronous time, so the narrative often interrupts one story to tell another, the threads of which have already been laid or will be picked up later. This story of God with the name El Shaddai, this story of The Breasted One's intervention in the fleshly affairs of women and their wombs, is interrupted by the story of the wife and daughters of Abraham's cousin, Lot, which takes place in and around Sodom and Gomorrah.

A brief sketch includes the opening lines, in which Lot is sitting in the doorway of the gate of the city (in contrast to Abraham sitting in the doorway of his tent), the destruction of the two cities, and Lot's wife looking back and turning into a pillar of salt. If we are meant to take biblical tales as cautionary, this account clearly says, "Don't look back at destruction. Keep going. Looking back can paralyze you."

Lot's daughters, who don't look back, survive and live in a cave with their father. Thinking they are the only people left on earth and feeling responsible for repopulating the planet, they decide to get their father drunk and have sex with him—one on each successive evening. They both become pregnant. The elder delivers a son, Moab, and the younger a son named Benammi. All this is recorded with no judgment or comment. Finger pointing is out, as far as the Spirit is concerned. The daughter's actions introduce a matriarchal line we will see later in the Bible. Ruth, a female descendent of Moab, is to be the great-grandmother of David, the king and psalmist. There may be speculation on the account of Sodom and Gomorrah and Lot's daughters, but several things are clear: biblical women take things into their own hands, and it is important to look forward rather than back.

Back to the Future

As one continues to read through to Genesis 20, the story cuts back to Abraham and Sarah, who is still beautiful at ninety despite her earlier protestations about being "waxed old." There is a reprise of the earlier account of the couple passing Sarah off to a ruler as a sister. This time the *ruah Elohim*—perhaps because the men become impotent—has shut or closed up the wombs of the king's entire household. The Spirit of Creation gives the king, Abimelech (meaning "my Father is King") a dream, explaining that Abraham is a prophet and is married to Sarah.

Confronted by the king, Abraham explains his misrepresentation by saying that he didn't think God was in this kingdom. He adds that Sarah is his half-sister. Abraham then prays to God and the women's wombs are reopened. Again the couple comes out with no punishment or chiding from Divinity, and Abimelech says to Sarah (not to Abraham), "I have given your brother a thousand pieces of silver"—and he adds, "You are completely vindicated." No guilt, no blame or shame for the woman Sarah. And then God singles out Sarah and does for her as was spoken. Sarah conceives. Isaac is delivered.

God and Wombs

At this point in Genesis there can be no question that conception is unmistakably the province of this Creator *ruah Elohim*, thy Shield, El-roi, El Shaddai. So too are life, protection, direction, and promises that will be kept. Whereas Eve's experience carries a curse, Sarah's is blessed. And whereas Sarah once worried what others thought, once believed she would be a laughingstock if she delivered a child in her nineties, now she rejoices as she plays with the word *laugh*. She says, "God hath made me to laugh, so that all that hear will laugh with me" (Genesis 21:6).

Things change quickly. Hagar becomes a problem to Sarah and hence Ishmael to Isaac, and Sarah asks Abraham to get rid of them. It breaks Abraham's heart. He is grieved. In fact, it is Sarah who is the first to figure out what is to be done in a very rocky situation—send the slave girl and her son away. It is at this emotional low point for a conflicted and grieved Abraham that—in a complete reversal of what is generally thought of male-female relations in the Bible—The Breasted One tells him to obey his wife: "Whatever Sarah says to you, obey her voice . . ." (Genesis 21:12).

"And Abraham rose early in the morning and took bread and water and gave them to Hagar and gave her the child and sent her away through the wilderness of Beer-sheba" (Genesis 21:14). This Spirit of God, which for a moment seems so forbidding and strict, has promised this grieving father that this son shall become a great nation.

Wilderness Experience

At this point in the story Sarah, the mother of Judaism and Christianity, and Abraham, the father of Judaism, Christianity, and Islam, are at home in a muddle with Isaac, and Hagar, the mother of Islam, is wandering with her child in the wilderness of Beer-sheba (the Well of the Oath). And it is with Hagar and the child that

God is verbally present, as She is with countless powerless biblical women. Hagar's water is gone, and she casts her son under one of the shrubs and goes a good way off because she cannot bear to see the death of her child. She lifts up her voice and weeps. To all appearances she and her child are serious victims. Marrying Abram was done in obedience to Sarai. Bearing a child was done in obedience to an angel of the Lord. Now, she is sitting weeping in the wilderness with her child, who she fears is near death. It's a stark moment.

A link between mothers and children is indicated in the text. While she cries, "God heard the voice of the lad" (Genesis 21:17).

Nothing has been said about the child crying or speaking. The mother's tears do get God's attention: ". . . and God's messenger calls out from the heavens and says to her 'What troubles you, Hagar? Fear not, for God has heard the cry of the boy where he is. Rise, Lift up the boy and hold him by the hand for I will make a great nation of him'" (Genesis 21:17–19 JPS).

Seeking and Finding

And God opens her eyes. She sees what she did not see before. A well of water is there. First, her crying need; second, the removal of fear; third, seeing the need fulfilled. The Spirit of God, *ruah Elohim*, has moved on the face of the waters for the entire cosmos in Genesis 1 and in an individual way for Hagar and her child.

If Hagar, in her extreme circumstance, couldn't remember that she had earlier seen an angel who told her not to fear, and if she couldn't remember that she saw God and God saw her, then perhaps we should not be too hard on ourselves when we fall apart. Perhaps we should write "Fear not" on our doorposts and key chains, and in our hearts.

The Mountaintop View

The story in chapter 22 in the first twenty verses of Genesis has been known throughout most of recorded time and around the world as the binding or the sacrifice of Isaac. Instead, the idea that God demands human sacrifice dies in this story. The idea that when God is Seen, children are protected, comes to the forefront of thought. The account is so profound and so laden with meaning that each detail unfolds the meanings implicate in the text. Once more Abraham is told to *lekh lekha*—get up and go—as he was told to leave his father's house when we first met him in chapter 12. These are the only two times we are told Abraham hears those words from God.

Once more "Abraham rose up early in the morning," as he did when he sent Ishmael and Hagar to the wilderness. This time he is to take Isaac to Moriah (Seen of God), up to a mountain for a burnt offering.

A surface reading of Genesis 22:1–19 makes it easy to see why some avoid the God they think is an angry, vengeful, demanding biblical Father God, who tempts His favorite person on earth by requiring a sacrifice of his son. As in the simpler account of Abraham in the door of his tent in the woods of Mamre, this story demands a deeper reading, with all that one has glimpsed about the *ruah Elohim*—the Shield, The Breasted One, El Shaddai—whose concerns have been conception, life, seeds, water, stars, protection, promises, and blessings.

By the time this tale unfolds, Abraham and Sarah have had much practice in trusting God. They left their ancestral home and found a fuller, richer life. God has already taken care of Ishmael. Abraham has a certain confidence in his relationship to God. Everything El Shaddai has told him to do has worked out to Abraham's benefit.

"Take your son, your only one, whom you love, Isaac, and go forth to the land of Moriah . . ." (Genesis 22:2). (Robert Alter's translation points out that God's "your only one" is significant, as Ishmael is also Abraham's son.)

The story of this almost sacrifice is fraught with symbols and prefigurations. And it must be read through those symbols to see what the story—other than the traditional, literal, and overly simplistic "Abraham had faith in God"—is saying. Again we are taken back to the third day of Creation by *ruah Elohim*, when on the third day of his journey Abraham raises his eyes and sees a sanctuary. There is a shift into another dimension, and this entire process takes place in the land of "Seen of God."

When questioned by his son, Abraham says that God will provide a lamb for the burnt offering, which is what happens when Abraham, just like Hagar in the wilderness, hears the voice of the messenger of God and lifts his eyes to see what he has not seen—a ram in a thicket. "And Abraham called the name of that place Jehovah-jireh: as it is said to this day, In the mount of the Lord it shall be seen" (Genesis 22:14).

The story says, go up to the mountain (the high place) and it "shall be seen." Not "go up to the mountain for a useless trip." Not "go up to the mountain and have your heart broken," or "go up to the mountain and kill your child." Abraham then goes and dwells at Beer-sheba ("the Well of the Oath")—where Hagar and Ishmael were nurtured and saved. The story of saving—not sacrifice—has come full circle.

Both Abraham's sons are intact, cared for by The Breasted One, and the stories are told so that there is no doubt of either the differences or the similarities. Some may wonder what Sarah was doing when her husband and son went to the mountain. If one thinks she was a powerless piece of property, she must have been anguished. But if one assumes that she knew, from experience, that God takes care of every detail, she was not worried.

Not the End of the Story

Years later, when Sarah dies, Abraham weeps and wails for her. Though in Genesis 23:19 her body is buried near Mamre at Machpelah, her name lives on in the Bible:

> That is, They which are the children of the flesh, these are
> not the children of God: but the children of the promise

are counted for the seed. For this is the word of promise,
At this time will I come, and Sarah shall have a son.
(Romans 9:8–9)

Fulfilled promise. New birth. Nothing is impossible to Spirit.
Creation revealed to complex human consciousness regardless of
gender. That's the story of Sarah, Hagar, and Abraham. It is a story
that lives today.

4

A Gathering of Women

And Jacob kissed Rachel, and lifted up his voice, and wept.
—Genesis 29:11

What in the present culture leads us to think that biblical women are veiled, isolated nonentities in a desert landscape, trailing behind husbands who are worshipping a vengeful male God? In fact, *Elohim*—The Breasted One, El Shaddai, The Existing One—sweeps through the accounts of the lives of the matriarchs who have their own relationships to God, legal and spiritual rights, and the same Spirit of God of the men of that time. In the Genesis 24 narrative of Rebekah, the King James Version uses the term *Lord God*—again giving the sense the God is male—whereas the Hebrew uses *The Existing One*, with definitions "to be, become, to become like, come to pass, exist." To "be and to become like" appears to echo the *ruah Elohim*: male and female created in our image. The lives of biblical women help make plain the female, mothering, spiritual aspect of the Divine.

Demythologizing Eve is not done in a single stroke. Part of the process of the demythologizing of Eve and the role and nature of women in the Bible is to search out the connections, histories, and experience of biblical women and to rediscover the Mother and Spirit aspect of the God of Abraham, Isaac, and Jacob.

We see reminders of that *ruah Elohim* of the first chapter of Genesis with Spirit on the face of the waters when we meet Rebekah at a well. A well is a micro version of the waters of Creation, but so many significant transformative biblical meetings take place at a well that we look, too, for the spiritual meaning. In the context of Creation we can see that the Spirit moves at the otherwise mundane and necessary location of a well. We see also that the woman—Rebekah—has the right to decide who and when she marries, to prophesy about her children, and to direct a son's marriage and the future of both her sons. Rebekah is the central human player in chapters 24 through 28 of Genesis. Creation is the context.

Rebekah is not an isolated, solitary figure in a desert landscape; rather, she appears as part of a prophecy that will involve generations. She enters the scene just after Sarah dies and is buried, and as part of a larger plan. Rebekah is also involved in the riveting parts of human life—sex, money, and in-laws.

Here is a short form of her story.

Finding a Wife

After Sarah's burial, Abraham sends his emissary to Mesopotamia, the land of Sarah's sister-in-law, Milcah, to find a wife for Isaac. Abraham tells his emissary in detail that an angel will go before him to find the right woman. The emissary offers an elaborate prayer to the God of Abraham that this will be so.

When he arrives, the emissary details to The Existing One what the so-far unknown woman will say and do. "May it be that when I say to a girl, 'Please let down your jar that I may have a drink,' and she says, 'Drink, and I'll water your camels too'—let her be the one you have chosen for your servant Isaac" (Genesis 24:14 NIV).

Simultaneously, Rebekah appears.

We can picture her only as being like the majority of women in the world today, of medium height, slightly rounded, brown skinned, with dark hair. We do know that she was very fair to look at. She offers the emissary exactly the kindnesses he has detailed—in exactly the words he has used in his prayer. She gives him water and waters the camels too, and he gives her a golden earring and two heavy gold bracelets.

From Genesis to Revelation the Bible repeats the placing of woman at the right time in the right location—synchronous time meeting chronological time. Abraham's emissary asks Rebekah whose daughter she is, and she gives him her father's and grandmother's names, adding that there is straw and feed at home and room for him to spend the night. In Genesis 24:26–28 the emissary bows his head and worships God:

> And he said, Blessed be the Lord God of my master Abraham, who hath not left destitute my master of his mercy and his truth: I being in the way, the Lord led me to the house of my master's brethren.
> And the damsel ran, and told them of her mother's house these things.

The Bible makes plain that the household is that of Rebekah's mother. These chapters of Genesis are about matriarchy and the Spirit of God moving in the lives of the women. The men play important parts, but the protagonists are women, as can be seen in countless biblical stories in countless continuing chapters and verse. Although the emissary recounts what Abraham has said to him and his progress in following Abraham's instructions, tells of Abraham's God and Abraham's prosperity showers gifts upon the household, and reiterates his prayers to God, the final point of this part of Rebekah's story will be her decision whether to marry Isaac:

> And her brother and her mother said, Let the damsel abide with us a few days, at the least ten; after that she shall go.
> And he said unto them, Hinder me not, seeing the Lord hath prospered my way; send me away that I may go to my master.
> And they said, We will call the damsel, and inquire at her mouth.
> And they called Rebekah, and said unto her, Wilt thou go with this man? And she said, I will go. (Genesis 24:55–58)

They invoke a blessing—in full awareness of the "curse" on Eve and the hatred in that story between the serpent and the seed of the woman.

"And they blessed Rebekah, and said unto her, Thou art our sister, be thou the mother of thousands of millions, and let thy seed possess the gate of those which hate them" (Genesis 24:60). This verse is another reference to the triumph of woman's seed over hatred, first described in the story of Eve. Reading only the first half of the first book of the Bible, we find references to the ultimate triumph of woman over hatred.

What Is Seen

Isaac is taking a walk in the field in the evening to meditate and lifts up his eyes. One simple biblical sentence indicates, in this most self-referential Book, that the evening and the morning were the *first day*; that, like his father Abraham meditating in the door of his tent before the angels or the Lord appears, his sight is elevated to another dimension. He sees camels coming. Rebekah, riding one of those camels, lifts up her eyes and sees Isaac.

He sees camels.

She sees him.

Rebekah, the story says, goes with Isaac into Sarah's tent—this is a story about matriarchs. "And he loved her; and Isaac was comforted after his mother's death" (Genesis 24:67). A single biblical sentence speaks volumes about their relationship.

Rebekah has a husband who loves her. There is no mention whether or not she, in return, loves him. She will have a monogamous marriage until her death.

Biology Again

The narration says that Rebekah is barren, as Sarah was barren. Isaac "pleaded" or "intreated" to The Existing One (Genesis 25:21).

Like returns like, and Rebekah conceives. Robert Alter, in his book *Genesis*, says and translates, that the children clash within her. "This that, the one, the other" we are told she asks The Existing One, or "Then why me?"

And The Existing One answers:

Two nations in your womb
Two peoples from your loins shall issue
People over people shall prevail,
The elder the younger's slave. (Robert Alter translation)

Rebekah's direct question to her God is an answered prophecy that she will understand and act upon as the twins grow. And although the assumption given by a reading of the King James Version is that Esau, the hairy one, is the firstborn and should have those rights, the Hebrew, according to Alter, is ambiguous as to which noun is subject and which object: the elder shall serve the younger, or the elder, the younger shall serve. Rebekah, however, already knows.

The child following Esau and holding his heel is named Jacob, which has a similarity to the word *heel*. Jacob will be described as a "plain man," meaning complete, perfect, one who lacks nothing in physical strength, beauty. The same word will later be associated with the man Job in his encounters with the female aspect of God.

In yet another description of the relationship of Isaac and Rebekah, "Isaac loved Esau, because he did eat of his venison: but Rebekah loved Jacob" (Genesis 25:28). This short description is another biblical example of human nature captured in a few bittersweet, poignant words.

Esau sells his "firstborn" birthright to Jacob for a pot of lentils, as he says he is starving and needs to eat the dinner Jacob had prepared. This scene leads into another in which there is a famine in the land and Isaac replays the sister-brother scene with the neighboring king Abimelech, as did his father Abraham before him. But

Isaac prospers, as did his father, and it is not until Esau marries Judith and Basemath—Hittite women—that Isaac and Rebekah see things the same way.

According to Alter's translation, "The newlyweds are a provocation to them—caused them grief of mind." In short: there is daughter-in-law trouble.

Strategies for Survival

Isaac still prefers Esau. Isaac is going to give him the birthright of the firstborn in exchange for venison, as Esau gave up his birthright for a pot of lentils. Rebekah steps up, mindful of the prophecy made while she was pregnant. At her urging ("Do what I say," she says) and with her full support, Jacob puts a hairy skin over his body. Isaac now has failing eyesight. He seems to have lost any spiritual vision he may have had and does not "lift up his eyes" as he did years before.

Although Rebekah's instincts and actions are in line with The Existing One, Jacob has denied his own identity. Pretending to be Esau in order to gain primogeniture will bring Jacob to the struggle for his spiritual identity. As a consequence of his actions he will spend years being deceived, even as he has deceived. And when Esau—like Adam and Eve's first son, Cain—decides to kill his brother, Rebekah hears of it before it can happen.

Readers of the story know that Esau's plan will fail because neither Adam nor Eve nor their children are the models for the children of The Existing One. Rebekah, who knows this at some level, has been, like Sarah before her, involving herself in the protection of her children by separating them. As a protection she sends Jacob to her brother Laban's. She does this by telling her husband that she is tired of her daughters-in-law and that she'd rather be dead than see Jacob have a wife like Esau's. Compounding the complication, Esau then marries the daughter of Ishmael—granddaughter of Hagar.

Marriage and Crucifixion

Jacob is following his mother's suggestion to his father and is on the way to seek a wife from Rebekah's premarital home. He lies down to sleep:

> And he dreamed, and behold a ladder set up on the earth, and the top of it reached to heaven: and behold the angels of God ascending and descending on it. And, behold, the Lord stood above it, and said, I am the Lord God of Abraham thy father, and the God of Isaac: the land whereon thou liest, to thee will I give it, and to thy seed. (Genesis 28:13)

Again, the King James Version uses Lord God when it could just as well be translated The Existing One. The King James Version also uses *ladder* when perhaps *ramp* would be more fitting but is not as poetic a word or image.

Marriage as Crucifixion

And then Rachel appears. Her story is as compelling as any in the Bible. Hers is not just a story of love at first sight. It is that, but it's more—duplicity, money, mandrakes, sex, maids, childbearing, and death—not just a story about a docile young piece of property who becomes mother to two sons of Jacob. It's a soap opera with enduring consequences. The story of Rachel is a story with timeless elements: love, sacrifice, rebirth, and more love. All these elements appear again in the account of her son Joseph to come.

Rachel's story begins in Genesis 29, when Jacob arrives at a well and sees three flocks of sheep, a huge stone over the mouth of the well, and Rachel, who is a shepherdess by profession.

> When Jacob saw Rachel, the daughter of Laban his mother's brother, and the sheep of Laban his mother's brother, that

Jacob went near, and rolled the stone from the well's mouth, and watered the flock of Laban his mother's brother.

And Jacob kissed Rachel, and lifted up his voice, and wept. (Genesis 29:10–11)

The Plot Thickens

"And Laban had two daughters: the name of the elder was Leah, and the name of the younger was Rachel. Leah was tender eyed; but Rachel was beautiful and well favoured. And Jacob loved Rachel; and said, I will serve thee seven years for Rachel thy younger daughter" (Genesis 29:16–18).

The story of this deception is widely known. After seven years and a veiled wedding night it is Leah, the firstborn, and not the younger Rachel who is in Jacob's bed. It is to be seven days— the complete set of the days of Creation by *ruah Elohim*—before Rachel and Jacob consummate their love. But for Jacob it is seven more years as a servant in Laban's house.

There is much maneuvering between the sisters and then their handmaids, Zilpah and Bilhah. For most, the situation can only be imagined. Four women, one husband, assorted children, a scheming father, mandrakes in exchange for a night with Jacob, a clash of cultures—it's a struggle for moral, spiritual, and legal rights, as well as a soap opera ripe with speculative possibilities.

Leah names her firstborn Reuben: Look, a son—"for she said, Surely the Lord hath looked upon my affliction; now therefore my husband will love me." But he does not. Hoping after each of three births that now her husband will love her, after the birth of Judah, a fourth son, Leah says, "Now will I praise the Lord" (Genesis 29:32). And she "gives off childbearing." Does this mean that she recognizes The Existing One, not her husband, as the source of her childbearing and her happiness?

Though loved to the hilt by her husband, Rachel is jealous of Leah's children and, echoing Rebekah's dramatic plea to her husband, asks Jacob for children, "or I will die!" But Jacob—unlike his father, Isaac, who entreated The Existing One on Rebekah's behalf—asks rather, "Can I take the place of God who has denied you fruit of the womb?" (Genesis 30:2 NAB).

"Fruit of the womb" is used in both Hebrew translations and in the King James Version. There are levels of interpretation to Jacob's statement. It can be read as a defensive, cutting remark, an instruction from one closer to God, or an indication that the womb is Creation, and that Rachel, as the image and likeness of this feminine *ruah Elohim*, has dominion over her experience. She, however, seems to recognize this only in steps, and she sends her husband to her maid. Bilhah conceives and conceives again. Then Rachel marks the wrestling that is going on (and that is to come for Jacob) when she says, "With great wrestlings have I wrestled with my sister, and I have prevailed" (Genesis 30:8).

More children by the maids—Rachel trades mandrakes or aphrodisiacs with Leah for nights with Jacob as Esau traded his birthright for lentils. Two more sons and a daughter for Leah, and by this time in the narrative we are deep, deep into complications when "And God remembered Rachel" (Genesis 30:22). Joseph is born. God remembered Noah in the rainbow covenant. We find this same rainbow remembering in the image of Joseph's coat of many colors and still later when we meet Hannah, one of the seven woman prophets of Israel. *Barren, fruit, womb, remember, conceive*—these words signal the process and presence of The Existing One on earth, in the flesh.

Third and Seventh Days

Not only has the remembering of The Existing One brought Joseph to earth, but Jacob now remembers home and wants to leave Laban's household and return to his own land. In the process, God—with an intriguing new appellation, "I am the God of Bethel"—speaks to Joseph.

Jacob first consults with Rachel and Leah. When Rachel and Leah are consulted, they are united. The jealousy associated with an acute sense of lack of power over one's own life has disappeared. Consulted and united, with decision-making power over their future, the sisters encourage and insist that Jacob "follow I am the God of Bethel." They all flee, Rachel with her father's household gods. It is three days before Laban discovers the group is gone, and seven more before he overtakes them.

> And God came to Laban the Syrian in a dream by night, and said unto him, Take heed that thou speak not to Jacob either good or bad. (Genesis 31:24)

"Ah, human nature" is all one can sigh when Laban finds the group and purports to be innocently wronged because they all went off without saying goodbye. But what he really wants to know is what happened to his household gods. Rachel has not told Jacob that she brought them along, and to hide them she sits on them and apologizes to the searching Laban for not getting up because she has her monthly period. This story, in Genesis 31:30–35, continues the deception practiced by Laban, although for now it is Laban who is deceived.

Israel

Rebekah, when the twins were wrestling in her womb, received prophetic news from The Existing One on the future of her children (Genesis 25:22–23). Rachel, her daughter-in-law, has said, "With great wrestling have I wrestled with my sister, and I have prevailed" (Genesis 30:8). Jacob still has his wrestling in front of him. There is still a loose end: the brother Esau (Genesis 32:3).

He is met on his way by *Elohim*—translated in the King James Version as angels of God, in Hebrew as messengers of God—but when Jacob addresses this entity or entities he says "You, Yourself" (Genesis 32:1).

In short order Jacob sends messengers to Esau saying that he wants to find grace in his sight, hears back that Esau has four hundred men, and is greatly distressed by the news; he divides his families and possessions into two groups to potentially spare the mothers and children from violence; he prays to El Shaddai, the God of his fathers, Abraham and Isaac; and he sends gifts to Esau. He then takes Rachel and Leah, the two handmaids, and all his children and crosses the river that runs between the Dead Sea and the Sea of Galilee—"And Jacob was left alone" in one of the central turning points of Scripture (Genesis 3:24). Rachel has already wrestled and prevailed. Now, after decades of in-laws, wives, maids, and children and the ghost of Esau, Jacob is left alone.

Turning Point

Here begins a seminal biblical story. That the man was left alone is a reminder that each individual works out a relationship to The Existing One, alone. "And there wrestled a man with him til the break of day"—until the light breaks (as in "Let there be light") (Genesis 32:24).

> And he said, Let me go, for the day breaketh. And he said, I will not let thee go, except thou bless me.
>
> And he said unto him, What is thy name? And he said, Jacob.
>
> And he said, Thy name shall be called no more Jacob, but Israel: for as a prince hast thou power with God and with men, and hast prevailed.
>
> And Jacob asked him, and said, Tell me, I pray thee, thy name. And he said, Wherefore is it that thou dost ask after my name? And he blessed him there.
>
> And Jacob called the name of the place Peniel: for I have seen God face to face, and my life is preserved.
> (Genesis 32:26–30)

Jacob struggles and finds his own identity and God.

Jacob and Esau are reconciled. Together they will bury their father.

Many from One

Jacob's name change to Israel is momentous. Biblical references to "Israel" are going to be more than references to one man. They will now refer to a whole group of people. A people—women and men—who, like Jacob, will bless and be blessed, deceive and be deceived, go astray and be led back, and wrestle with themselves and who they are until the moment they discover their real, uncompromised spiritual identity. "Children of Israel" is not only a reference to the descendants of Jacob but also a metaphor for the person who goes through the struggle with self and recognizes God.

Moving On

And God appears again to Jacob, saying: "I am El Shaddai. Be fruitful and multiply" (Genesis 35:11 TNK). This Breasted One is translated in the King James Version as God Almighty. Clearly, fertility and multiplication are aspects of the Spirit of God in the first chapter of Genesis, whereas God Almighty bears the magisterial tone of King James—not the abundant tone of the Hebrew, El Shaddai.

As she has prophesied, Rachel becomes pregnant again. The household sets out from Bethel. Rachel is in labor. When her labor is the hardest the midwife tells her to have no fear, she is having another boy. "But as she breathed her last, for she was dying, she named him Benomi; but his father called him Benjamin. Thus Rachel died." She is buried "in the way of Ephrath, which is Bethlehem" (Genesis 35:16–18 TNK).

Again, "have no fear" or "fear not" are the biblical injunctions to women. Some translations use the word *travail* for labor. *Travail* is the word used in the King James Version in conjunction with the woman in Revelation pursued by the great red dragon. Whether we read *travail* or *labor* does not change the essential female imagery. But the biblical use of *travail* for "birth pangs" means the contractions are not just localized, but generic to delivering an idea to earth—to human consciousness.

As we read Rachel's story in Genesis 35:19, we read that Jacob buried Rachel "in the way of Ephrath, which is Bethlehem." Rachel's dying in childbirth is not merely the end of one matriarch's story. It is the fertile ground from which another story of mother and child springs. Bethlehem is where Mary will give birth to Jesus. Again, the Bible is self-referential. The lives of the women in the Bible are connected and interwoven in birth, life, death, and birth again, and connect to the people as a whole. The prophet Jeremiah illustrates another association: "A voice is heard in Ramah, lamentations, and bitter weeping; Rachel weeping for her children refused to be comforted for her children, because they are not" (Jeremiah 31:15). *Ramah* is a feminine noun suggesting "high place." In Ramah, this high place, the prophet Deborah will judge Israel. Yet another prophet, Hannah, will conceive in Ramah, and that child, Samuel, will be buried in Ramah.

Wives, not husbands, are the focus of the last of the major genealogies in Genesis 36, which begins with Esau, and the list of who has the children proceeds primarily from the wives and not the husband. The women in Genesis are the agents for change.

On the Way to Egypt

The journey of Israel to Egypt is depicted through the story of Rachel's eldest son, Joseph. The tale of his coat of many colors, reflecting the rainbow, is one of the most familiar biblical stories. Joseph is his father's favorite son. He tells his dreams before he has figured them out. Hatred and jealousy drive the ten sons of Leah, Bilhah, and Zilpah to drop Joseph into a dry well. There is no water there. They mean for Joseph to die.

While the brothers are eating they lift up their eyes, moving the story into another dimension. They see some of Ishmael's descendants coming toward them on camels. It is Judah who suggests that instead of leaving Joseph to die in a dry well, they should sell him into slavery. As in any respectable page-turner, this chapter leaves the protagonist in ambiguous circumstances. His father is told that he is dead, but he is alive, though not free, in Egypt, a slave in the house of the chief steward of Pharaoh. We are left wondering what might happen to him, because a woman, Tamar, becomes the focus of the next biblical story.

Tamar

Tamar turns the male law upside down. Her story, in chapter 38 of Genesis, reverses another misconception—that if a woman does not have children she is replaced. In Tamar's story the men are replaced. She is clever and resourceful, the matriarch of the line of which David will become king. The story's focus is Tamar—what she is entitled to and how she gets her entitlement. Her story continues the biblical evolution of thought that takes away the curse on Eve.

Again the story starts with a man—in this case, Judah, who has suggested slavery rather than death for Joseph. He leaves his brothers, but by the second sentence of the account he marries the daughter of Shua, who conceives and names her three sons. Tamar is chosen as a wife for his first-born son. That son dies, and Judah tells Onan, his second son, to marry Tamar and fulfill the law of levirate marriage and provide children for the dead brother's line.

Onan does not fulfill that obligation, and he too dies (Genesis 38:8–10). Judah has participated in what might be the death of his brother, and now two of his sons die. Judah, still adhering to or mindful of that levirate law, tells Tamar to go to her father's house and stay a widow until his third son, Selah, grows up—"for he thought, Lest peradventure he die also, as his brethren did" (Genesis 38:11).

Judah does not keep his promise to send the third son. Tamar takes action. She leaves her father's house, puts off her widow's garments, covers herself with a veil, and sits in an open place by the way. When Judah sees her, he takes her for a harlot and asks to sleep with her. She says, "What wilt thou give me, that thou mayest come in unto me?" (Genesis 38:16). He promises her a kid from his flock, and in the exchange she asks for a pledge until he sends the kid—his seal and cord and the staff he carries. Burning with sexual desire, he gives them to her. She conceives.

Judah does send a kid in exchange for the symbols of his identity and power, but no one can find the harlot. Further, all the men of the town (who would apparently know) say there was no prostitute working that spot on the road. Three months later, Judah hears that Tamar has played the harlot and that she is with child by harlotry. Still stuck in the male sense of the law, Judah says, "let her be burned" (Genesis 38:24 TNK). Here again is hatred of the woman and her seed for violating male ordinances. Later in the Bible the prophets will use the word *harlot* as a political term for nations straying from God.

Tamar arrives at Judah's and sends him the symbols of his authority—the seal, cord, and staff—saying she is pregnant by the man who owns them. Stopped short, Judah reverses his position and says that, by default, Tamar "is more in the right than I" (Genesis 38:26 TNK). Judah did not keep his promise to send her the third son. And he is not intimate with her again. Rather than waiting in line, Tamar waited "in the way." Judah has served his immediate purpose in Tamar's life.

The ramifications of Tamar's story are manifold. Without her, the name Judah would not appear—as it does—823 times in the Bible. The name appears first as the son of the mother who named him, then associated with the woman he has selected for his first son, then in reference to the tribe of Judah, to his children, their children, the land, and on into prophecy and the Book of Revelation.

Who Is to Judge?

Lot's daughters and Tamar, Sarah, and Rebekah—and more biblical women to come—take matters into their own hands. There is no judgment on Lot's daughters, and Tamar is more righteous than the male head of the line of Judah. In the Hebrew Bible and in the New Testament Gospels to come, the texts make clear that *ruah Elohim*, The Existing One, overturns male law and is on the side of women who might otherwise be powerless.

Tamar gives birth to twins, as did Rebekah. Through her encounter with Judah she is mother to the line of children who carry on through the male line to Boaz. Boaz will marry Ruth, a descendant of the incestuous relationship between the daughters of Lot and their father. Boaz and Ruth are the great-grandparents of David, the king. Their names also appear in the biological genealogy of Jesus.

Joseph

Whereas Tamar's tale portrayed sex in the service of procreation, here the Bible cuts back to Joseph and a woman who wants to seduce him—and procreation is not the issue. She is an Egyptian, the wife of Joseph's master. He rejects her advances. Joseph may be a dreamer, but he is trustworthy. Nevertheless, he is thrown into prison (Genesis 39:6–23).

Through many adventures, Rachel's son Joseph makes his way through prison, where his ability to interpret dreams saves him and eventually places him second only to Pharaoh. In this position of power he gives grain to his brothers, whose father Israel (Jacob) has sent them down to Egypt when there is famine in their own land. After more deceptions, this time on the part of Joseph, Israel and his entire family join Joseph in Egypt (Genesis 42–47:27).

Israel's twelve sons are now the heads of the twelve tribes of Israel, and on his deathbed their father gathers them together and dissects their characters as he prophesies. It is a must read to understand what happens to each of the individual tribes. Looking at what Jacob says about each of his sons and remembering what their mothers named them, the contrast is illuminating.

Biblical names have meanings and carry allusions. They are meant to alert the reader to deeper significance and to connections between people. Joseph, for example, is portrayed here as a nice man, a good man, a man who serves others and loves unconditionally. Biblically speaking, this background and the name are to be taken into consideration upon the introduction of Joseph, the husband of Mary, and of her child, Jesus. As numbers also have meaning and weave through Bible texts as signs, the number twelve appears again in the twelve stars on the crown of the woman in Revelation. There are twelve disciples, and there are twelve princes that descend from Ishmael.

Joseph is finally reconciled with his family. In a brilliant act of forgiveness and transformation, he says, "Besides, although you intended me harm, God intended it for good, so as to bring about the present result—the survival of many people" (Genesis 50:20 TNK).

And so the Israelites are in Egypt for 430 years, setting the stage for Miriam, sister of Aaron, and her brother Moses, for the Passover and for the parting of the Sea and yet another return to the ideas of spiritual Creation described in the first chapter of Genesis—a continuation of the Spirit of God moving on the face of the waters.

5

I Am That I Am

And the angel of God, which went before the camp of Israel,
removed and went behind them; and the pillar of the cloud
went from before their face, and stood behind them.
—Exodus 14:19

Spirit—that feminine plural word for Creator—is very much
present in the Book of Exodus. Spirit—with another new name, I
Am That I Am—is the cause of action throughout the account of
deliverance as both a personal and a national Deliverer. The Book
of Exodus is a study in the developing understanding of a living,
present, all-powerful, all-wise, saving Deity—remembering, hearing, seeing, and delivering not just one child, one couple, or two, or
twelve families, but a nation. And it is not all sweetness and light.
There is more *labor* and *travail* as well as triumph, as the Spirit of
God moving on the face of the water is everywhere in this story.

The story of the Exodus of the children of Israel from Egypt, of
Moses and the Ten Commandments, begins with remembering, as
it repeats the names of the twelve sons of Israel who went to Egypt
(Exodus 1:1–5). Though no sketch can do the Book of Exodus jus-
tice, we will remember here some of the substance of the drama of
Miriam, Moses, Aaron, and the children of Israel.

Then there rose up a new king in Egypt who "knew not Joseph"—
who does not remember (Exodus 1:8). The sentence is heartbreaking.

The Israelites have spent 430 years as guests in Egypt, but now
the king fears their increase in number, and he enslaves them. No
matter how much they are oppressed, their birthrate continues to
climb. Pharaoh, the king, orders all male babies to be killed at birth
by throwing them into the Nile River. This attempt at ethnic

cleansing—the consequences of one people's irrational fear of another—will, after much tribulation, fail. The oppressed will be delivered. The process of deliverance begins with women.

Women Deliver

Shriprah and Puah are the named midwives who brilliantly reflect the process of deliverance of the people, and whether they are merely two women or their names stand in for all the midwives to the Hebrews, the fact is that they save the male babies in defiance of Pharaoh. And one mother of a newborn male builds an ark, puts her infant son in that carrier, and sends him down the river. The text, and the words *ark* and *water*, make it clear that this is to be a repeat saving of all the people—as it was in the experience of Noah. The Spirit of God will move on the waters.

Pharaoh's daughter finds the baby in the ark. She has compassion and pity and spares him (Exodus 2:6). Now comes the sister of the baby (we later learn she is named Miriam, meaning well or water). She offers to find a good nursemaid for the child and calls their mother. Now the women—midwives, mother, Pharaoh's daughter, and the sister—have all been gathered to save the child. The mothering of the Spirit has moved on the face of the waters from delivery out of the womb to the ark to the river to compassion, to tears when the babe wept.

"And when she had opened it, she saw the child: and, behold, the babe wept. And she had compassion on him, and said, 'This is one of the Hebrews' children'" (Exodus 2:6). To punctuate that mothering of all Creation from the moving of the waters, Pharaoh's daughter later names the child "Moses, because I drew him out of the water" (Exodus 2:10).

Adventures in the Wilderness

In less than a sentence after he is named, Moses appears as a grown man; in the next sentence, he has killed an Egyptian he sees hitting a Hebrew. A mere five sentences more and Moses has fled from Pharaoh, who wants him killed. In the desert, sitting by a well, he meets the seven shepherdess daughters of the priest of Midian, who have come to draw water for their flock.

Here again we are in both the world of the literal and the world of symbol, reference, allusion, and spiritual definition. The *flock*, as in Rachel's story, is often used biblically to represent not just sheep but numbers of people. Seven not only is the sign of completeness represented by the seven days of Creation but also represents blessing.

Once again the self-referential nature of the Bible can be seen. The Bible's opening words are continually repeated in the lives of the characters. We are reminded of the spiritual Creation in Genesis in so many ways—names, numbers, and elements. Just the second chapter of the second book of the Bible so densely layers the stories that they become one narrative—even though happening in different eras to different individuals and peoples.

Layer upon Layer

Moses' encounter with the seven daughters at the well exemplifies the recurring biblical theme: how a man or men treat women has national and international repercussions. Shepherds are harassing the women at the well (Exodus 2:17–22). Moses rises up in their defense and "waters the flock"—an indication on a local scale of what he will do later on a national scale. He will stand up to Pharaoh as he stands up to the shepherds, helping the Hebrews leave Egypt as he helps the women. He will be with the women for forty years, as the children of Israel will wander in the desert for forty years. The man Moses' individual experience with the seven women is extrapolated to the experience of the people and the nation as a whole.

But in the midst of the grander themes, the Bible describes daily existence. The father of the women—who is a priest of Midian—asks them why they are home so early from work. They report that an Egyptian helped them. The father asks the daughters why they have left the man at the well, and they fetch him. "And Moses was content to dwell with the man; and he gave Moses Zipporah his daughter" (Exodus 2:21). The Bible text leaves unresolved whether Moses asked for Zipporah or she for him.

Much has been told in a short few verses of the Bible. Before the end of the second chapter of Exodus, *Elohim* has heard the *groaning* (a feminine case noun we shall see again) of the children of Israel and "God remembered his covenant with Abraham, with Isaac and with Jacob . . . and God had respect unto them" (Exodus 2:24–25). The rest of the story—trouble and departure from Egypt, the parting of the Sea, the continuing journey, the Ten Commandments, and new names for God—fills several chapters, beginning with Exodus.

The Burning Bush

The biblical God supersedes the science that deals with matter and energy as motion and force. Moses is on the mountain, Horeb. "An angel of the Lord appeared to him in a blazing fire out of a bush. He gazed, and there was a bush all aflame, yet the bush was not consumed" (Exodus 3:2 TNK). As in the earlier story of Hagar, first an angel appears, then God. Moses is afraid to look at the bush or God. The Existing One sees that Moses turns aside. Out of the burning bush Moses is called by name: "Moses. Moses" (Exodus 3:4). And he replies. "Here am I"—fully present mentally and geographically.

"The place whereon thou standest is holy ground," says God (Exodus 3:5). The holy ground is not a building built with hands or machinery, not a center of social and political events, but, in this case, a patch of ground on a remote mountain. The Existing One, The Breasted One is remembering and reminding as Moses hears: "I am thy God of thy father; the God of Abraham, the God of Isaac, and the God of Jacob" (Exodus 3:6).

Not abstract or distant, this Mothering Presence says of Israel, "I have seen, I have heard, I know its pain, I have come down to rescue." Moses has seen and heard and knows the pain of the

Hebrews, and he will, in mimetic pattern, come down to rescue the people of Israel.

He asks, in response, "Look, when I come to the Israelites and say to them, 'The God of your fathers has sent me unto you,' and they say to me 'What is his Name?' what shall I say to them?" (Exodus 3:8). The response is "'Ehyeh-'Asher-'Ehyeh, I Will Be Who I Will Be." Had Deity wanted to be known as a male God sitting on a throne, this mountaintop moment might have been the time to declare that. But no such declaration was made. Instead we have a profound, Divine explication. Robert Alter says that "rivers of ink have since flowed in theological reflection" on this response from Divinity. Whether read as "I Am That I Am"—as in the King James translation, bold, firm, and magisterial—or "I Will Be Who I Will Be," as in Tyndale and Alter, this is the name that God says "will be for all eternity."

I Will Be Who I Will Be instructs Moses to tell Pharaoh that the God of the Hebrews has met with them and "now, let us go three days into the wilderness, that we may sacrifice to our God" (Exodus 3:18). The designation of three days signals a return to the third day of Creation in chapter 1 of Genesis. The coming events in Egypt and the parting of the Red Sea signify Creation and the Spirit of God moving on the waters. Events are moving to another dimension.

Provision

More good news comes with the reminder that God provides—"ye shall not go out empty" (Exodus 3:21)—and that God's concern is inclusive. The Hebrews need not leave Egypt empty-handed. From Abraham to Hagar to Rachel and Leah to the Israelites in Egypt, for every injunction to leave there is a provision.

The Serpent and the Rod

Moses accepts the message on the mountain, but he fears that his people will not, and asks questions of I Will Be Who I Will Be, who speaks more in the third and fourth chapters of Exodus than so far in the Scriptures. "What is that in your hand?" (Exodus 4:2–4). A rod. The rod becomes a serpent—a reference to the serpent in the Garden of Eden. Moses grabs the serpent by the tail and it becomes a rod again. The serpent is an illusion.

Exodus tackles with and delivers the people from the serpent and Eden, displacing that misty creation of Genesis 2 with the absoluteness of the spiritual Creation of chapter 1. The theme of power over the serpent, the illusion, continues through the Bible and culminates in Revelation 12:3 in which the woman is pursued by the serpent swollen to a dragon but also about to "give birth to a man child who will rule with a rod of iron."

Power over Flesh

In case the sign and power of the rod isn't enough to illustrate the illusory nature of the senses, I Will Be Who I Will Be tells Moses to put his hand in his bosom. Moses pulls out the hand, covered with leprosy. He puts his hand back in his bosom and it is whole again— free of disease. From Exodus to the Psalms to Jeremiah and Isaiah, health and wholeness are conditions that God provides.

"I Am the Lord that healeth thee." Exodus 15:26 of the King James translation uses the I Am. "I Will Be Who I Will Be heals you" is another version of the same text.

> For I will restore health unto thee, and I will heal thee
> of thy wounds, saith the Lord. (Jeremiah 30:17)

> Then shall thy light break forth as the morning, and thine
> health shall spring forth speedily: and thy righteousness
> shall go before thee; the glory of the Lord shall be thy reward.
> (Isaiah 58:8)

The I Am on Horeb, whose name shall be forever, has power over the flesh (as over conception in earlier biblical chapters). This chimerical leprosy appears later on in Exodus when Miriam—unfairly, it seems to some—is struck with the disease (Numbers 12:10). Moses will ask, successfully, that she be healed.

Passover

Remembering is repeated. The story of the ten plagues visited upon Pharaoh and his people—the Pharaoh who, no matter how much he or his people may or may not want to let the Israelites go, has his heart hardened by the Omnipresent—is repeated yearly in the celebration of Passover, a script of living drama (Exodus 7:13–12:51). Passover is not just about the past but also about the here and now—addressing the consequences of personal and political action as well as exemption from suffering.

The plagues indicate the destruction of any power or belief antagonistic to spiritual Creation. John D. Currid, in his book *Ancient Egypt and the Old Testament*, outlines the Plagues as De-Creation; Plague nine—darkness prevailing over light—refers to day one of Genesis 1:6–8 when Light is created out of darkness. Currid's book continues elaborating on the plagues, contrasting to the six days of Creation in Genesis 1—a study some may want to pursue.

The Passover meal contains elements with symbolic value: lamb (Exodus 12:3), unleavened bread, bitter herbs. There are no instructions in Exodus as to the gender of the person leading the service at the memorial meal. The Passover meal is referred to throughout the Bible and is called the Last Supper of Jesus later in the Gospel texts.

Sea, Land, and the Third Day

Moses stretches his hand over the sea, and the children of Israel walk on dry land. In Genesis 1, on the third day of Creation the dry land appears, but only after the waters have been gathered together, as the seas have been gathered together. Clock time and simultaneous time meet—the sea parts. The dry land appears. Moses and the people are at one with *ruah Elohim*, El Shaddai, the Shield and Great Reward, The Existing One, I Will Be Who I Will Be.

The people live and are free. No oppressors are left to follow. The oppressors have disappeared in the remembrance and reenactment of the spiritual Creation in Genesis.

Women's Response

Now the people must deal with God alone. And one way they begin to do that is recorded: "And Miriam the prophetess, Aaron's sister, took the timbrel in her hand, and all the women went out after her in dance with timbrels. And Miriam chanted for them: 'Sing to the Lord, for He has triumphed gloriously, Horse and its driver He has hurled into the sea!'" (Exodus 15:20–21 TNK). Miriam's song will be echoed in part by Hannah, in 1 Samuel 2:1–11, in a further connection of biblical women.

Eagle's Wings

"They went on into the wilderness of Shur: they traveled three days in the wilderness and found no water. They came to Marah, but they could not drink the water of Marah because it was bitter; that is why it was named Marah" (Exodus 15:22–23).

In verses 22 and 23, just after Israel's passage through the Sea, Israel is also faced with the deprivation of three days with no water. Hard on the heels of joy is sorrow. A juxtaposition of joy and bitterness often reappears throughout the Bible—as it does in life.

Moses cries out to God, who shows him a piece of wood. Throwing the wood into the water changes the water from bitter to sweet. How this happens does not make much sense in the English language. Looking to the Hebrew root for *wood*—to make firm; hence to shut, especially the eyes—we can infer that the story is not about a patriarch who is shown a two-by-four piece of wood that somehow has miraculous, one-time power. It's not impossible to accept that the people's eyes are opened to the abundant provision of Spirit's Creation. Opening the eyes is a prerequisite to seeing God's provision, which is what happens when Ruth and Naomi appear on the biblical scene. Later, in the Book of Ruth, Naomi, widowed and with two sons dead, says "Call me not Naomi, call me Marah."

Chapter 19 of Exodus further expands the qualities of the many-named God: "You have seen what I did to the Egyptians, how I bore you on eagle's wings and brought you to Me" (Exodus 19:4 TNK). The foundation of God as Mothering and Fathering has been laid, from the Spirit moving on the face of the waters to the protection of the Ark, to the I Will Be Who I Will Be, the One who does all things—unlimited, impossible to confine, and presently here. In this Mothering and Fathering, in this movement of protection and definition of eternal, forever consciousness, preparation is made for the presentation of the Ten Commandments to the daughters and sons borne on the eagle's wings.

Protection and Prohibition

Some entertain the notion that the Commandments are a set of outdated prohibitions dropped down on stone by a vengeful, jealous male God to His appointed male spokesman. But the ground has been laid for the Mother and Father and All Being of God as the Primal Cause. Here is how the Commandments come to consciousness: "On the third day, as morning dawned, there was thunder, and lightning, and a dense cloud upon the mountain, and a very loud blast of the horn; and all the people who were in the camp trembled" (Exodus 19:16 TNK).

Attention must be paid to Exodus 20:1:

God spoke all these words, saying, I am the Lord your God who brought you out of the land of Egypt, the house of bondage. You shall have no other gods before Me.

Their experiences and a new understanding of the nurturing, caring, providing, ever-present nature of Spirit have led the children of Israel to this point. This Me is no longer a tribal God for just one family. This Me is Spirit—the One who made, makes, and does all things. The people are reminded of God through the Commandments. There is no escaping the call to remember who is who and what is what. There are reminders of the three realms of spiritual creation of Genesis 1 in the call to the Commandments (Exodus 20:1–17): "You shall make you no image of what is in the heavens above or in the earth below or the waters beneath the earth." And a reminder of the seventh day of Creation in: "Remember the sabbath day and keep it holy."

In a literal sense the Commandments are the organizing principles of these people. Now they are reminded to depend not on the authority of a king or judge but on individual response to Deity, the community, and self. Viewed not as prohibitions but as protection, the Commandments spare women and men the consequences of murder, theft, and adultery; alert them to the ravages of envy; and keep them from being assimilated in the land of "other" gods. Law, seated in individual behavior, protects both the individual and the community.

There is no statement from God that the Commandments are easy to live by. But they are part of the way out of slavery into a Promised Land. It takes meekness, as Moses was meek, to imbibe the Commandments. And, as the Decalogue does not seem easy to take at first glance, they are simply presented and then are commented on later—in great detail.

The Cloud and the Glory

Moses went all the way up into the mount, and a cloud covered the mount, and—in further commentary on the days of Creation outlined in the first chapter of Genesis—the Bible says:

And the glory of the Lord abode upon mount Sinai, and
the cloud covered it six days: and the seventh day he called
unto Moses out of the midst of the cloud. And Moses was
in the cloud forty days and forty nights. (Exodus 24:16)

The *glory* and the *cloud* are significant recurring themes from
Genesis to Revelation, though what is in the cloud and the text
may appear obscure to both the reader and the people below at the
foot of the mountain. In biblical texts both the words *cloud* and
glory often illustrate the feminine, in-dwelling presence of Spirit or
the Holy Spirit. In extra-biblical texts this Spirit is often referred to
as Shekinah (God's Presence). (A fuller discussion in reference
to Shekinah may be found at jewishencyclopedia.com, where
reference is made to Shekinah as a word interchangeable with
Elohim.) In biblical texts the term *Shekinah* is derived from the
Hebrew root *shakhan*, "To dwell, reside, abide."

Scholars also see similarities between Shekinah, The Holy
Spirit of God, the Hebrew *ruah Elohim*, the Greek Pneuma Hagion,
and the Hebrew Bat Kol ("The Daughter of the Voice," or God's
Voice). This cloud leads the Israelites by day and by night as a pillar of fire. They don't move without being led by the cloud. The
glory finds a home in the Tabernacle that the people work together
willingly to build.

The book of Exodus begins with the Hebrews forgotten in slavery. The journey out of slavery, out of Egypt, ends with remembering a feminine aspect of God in the very center of worship.

6

Rough Places, Plain Places

And they came, both men and women, as many as were willing hearted, and brought bracelets, and earrings, and rings, and tablets, all jewels of gold.

—Exodus 35:22

How does one get through the rough places in the Bible? Let's take a brief look at a few examples.

There are places in the Bible in which bad things happen to good or innocent people and places in which the marginal and unnamed are treated badly. There are passages so heavy with prescription and proscription that it is hard for the reader to tell at first glance what is going on. There are passages that seem strikingly inconsistent. And there are those passages that are dated, at best.

But more often than not, the Bible tells how marginal and unnamed people are treated better than kings and princes. And there are places in the text so clear, so inspired, and so familiar that they appear to be all the truth you have ever known.

There have been many explanations, many attempts at explanations of the rough places. Men and women have founded churches and formed denominations based on explanations of the rough places as well as on their inspired vision of biblical texts. But whether or not the reader finds a satisfying explanation on the first, second, or thousandth read (if that be the case) is up to the individual and the sense of revelation she has about the Scripture she has in front of her. Even that sense of revelation in a verse or story may take on more light, more focus as time glides by or as the eye and critical faculties become clearer.

Process and the Tabernacle

The building of the tabernacle (Exodus 25), although a favorite section for few readers, gives a glimpse into the methodology of some of the Bible and an indication of possible readings. Not a few people through the ages have explained the copious instructions for the tabernacle as a symbolic description of the universe. To those readers, chapter 31 verse 3 of Exodus, "I have filled them with the Spirit of God," echoes chapter 1 verse 2 of Genesis, "And the Spirit of God moved upon the face of the waters," and is an indication that something is going on here in the building of the tabernacle that relates to Creation.

Others feel even today that these are the actual instructions for building a sanctuary for the Lord. Still others think the instructions reflect the work it takes to develop a spiritual self. Aside from these constructions, it is clear that the specific detail involved in building the tabernacle serves as a break in the lives of the people so that consciousness does not dwell in nostalgia for the irreversible past or a desire to plunge into a fixed future.

The building of the portable tabernacle, which does not contain God, can be likened to reading the Bible. The Bible is portable— something once quite remarkable that we now take for granted. And Deity may be found not only between the actual covers or when scrolling on an Internet site, but in the very real process of searching, reading, meditating, acting on what is found there—in the weaving and joining and collecting and hammering down of disparate thoughts and ideas. In other words, as you read, study, put into practice what the Bible has to say to you, then you are building the tabernacle.

Instructions for building the tabernacle are given twice and broken up with a story in the middle: the building of the Golden Calf, which is a story of how not to and what not to build. The first set of instructions for building the tabernacle begins when Moses comes down from his forty days and nights on the mountain. Amid the details of construction, it is stated in Exodus 35:5 that the tabernacle is to be built equally by men and women; who works will be decided not by gender but by "whosoever is of a willing heart."

The women assemble at the door of the congregation as their mirrors are hammered down to make the laver in the center of the tabernacle. They are giving up a merely physical sense of beauty and self for a spiritual sense. The passage also indicates that a willingness to work on a project larger than oneself gives one a different identity.

The Golden Calf, the Tower of Babel, the Ark, and Solomon's temple are other things the Bible describes as being built. Some are at God's instructions, built for overall benefit. Comparing each biblical construction might be of interest to someone building a house, to an architect, to anyone who is interested in learning how to read a story on more than one level or anyone interested in patience and the value of process in human life. There is more to the seemingly tedious tabernacle section than meets the eye at first glance.

Rape, Dismemberment, and Murder

Certainly there are places in the Bible that many today may find hopelessly out of date. What you think of these sections may have something to do with where you are today in your own conscious path of disentangling opinion from fact. Though there are options that might be considered as a point of departure, it is ultimately up to the reader to find explanations for some of these passages. The Book of Judges is one such place.

The Book of Judges is full of difficult, rough places, and one reason that it has been considered difficult may be its illustration of women as the movers and shakers of action and central to biblical events. Taking a brief but closer look at some of Judges illustrates possible approaches to the rough places. In Judges are found most of the things that bother people about the Bible and about human life. Judges illustrates violence and horrible behavior. Be alerted, as you read, that the chronology of Judges doesn't always track in ways one might expect. And be warned again that there is violence, and violence against unnamed women. However, it is not an apology for the Bible to say that there is no more or less violence within its pages than today on television, in the movies, or on the streets and roads of countless cities and nations.

A glimpse of some of the texts shows that Judges itself says that all is not sweetness and light:

> In those days there was no king in Israel; every man did
> as he pleased. (Judges 17:6)

The last verse of the Book of Judges, 21:25, repeats this statement.

History and Metaphor

Returning to the first six verses of the Book of Judges, there is a war led by Judah and seemingly encouraged by God, at least ten thousand people are killed, and Adonibezek loses his thumbs and big toe. Such dismemberment is not just the gory, uncivilized past but continues today in tribal and religious and state-sponsored war. But is the point here that nothing changes? Or does this account warn us also, metaphorically, of the cutting apart, the fragmentation of the extremities of experience? And what are we to make of the verses in Judges 1:12–15, in which a woman given as a battle prize becomes one of the numbers of women who get the good they ask for and more. Achsah, this particular woman, receives not only good, but also a blessing, as Jacob received a blessing, and not only land, but springs of water—symbolizing life.

Women's History

Part of Judges, the story and song of Deborah, is thought by some to date from about the time of Genesis. Women's history has been with us as long as there has been history. But how to interpret that history has not been the province of women until recent centuries.

As you read, you will take part in the interpretation of this ancient manuscript in the light of today's experience.

> Deborah, wife of Lapidoth, was a prophetess; she led Israel
> at that time. She used to sit under the Palm of Deborah,
> between Ramah and Bethel in the hill country of Ephraim,
> and the Israelites would come to her for decisions.
> (Judges 4:4–5 TNK)

Have you ever accused a woman of being "too threatening"? If ever that were possible, Deborah is an example. The prophetess is a commander-in-chief and has an entire nation, people, and army at her disposal, plus the power of God to call men to her. And oddly enough, the name Lapidoth is a feminine noun in Hebrew meaning "torches" or perhaps "firebrand." Biblically speaking, Deborah (also the name of Rebekah's nurse) sits under the tree that stands between Ramah and Bethlehem. Ramah is where Rachel weeps for her children, and Bethel, where Jacob built an altar to the Spirit that renamed him Israel. There Deborah is—in the midst of the symbols of remembrance of both male and female, of transformation, of sorrow and joy.

Remembering that Deborah is part of a woman's heritage reminds us that women lead in the name of the biblical God and that women cannot legitimately be compartmentalized, marginalized, or stereotyped.

Deborah summons her general, Barak, and says to him: "The Lord God of Israel has commanded: Go, march up to Mount Tabor, and take with you ten thousand men of Naphtali and Zebulon. And I will draw Sisera, Jabin's army commander, with his chariots and his troops, toward you up to the Wadi Kison; and I will deliver him into your hands" (Judges 4:6–7 TNK).

He needs her.

> But Barak said to her, "If you will go with me, I will go;
> if not, I will not go."

"Very well, I will go with you," she answered. "However there will be no glory for you in the course you are taking, for then the Lord will deliver Sisera into the hands of a woman." (Judges 4:8–9 TNK)

Did Barak know better than to go without Deborah? Or is a female leader a necessity for final victory?

The whole of Judges 5 is called Deborah's song, although Barak also speaks or sings the verse. As you read that chapter, remember that it can be characterized in the female voice. Is it perhaps appropriate to read the whole song aloud to get the full import of women's strength and place in prophecy, and in national and international events?

Deborah sings in the King James translation: "The inhabitants of the villages ceased, they ceased in Israel, until that I Deborah arose, that I arose a mother in Israel." The Tanakh Hebrew translation of this verse in Judges 5:7 has this:

Deliverance ceased,
Ceased in Israel,
Till you arose, O Deborah,
Arose, O mother, in Israel!

When phrases from Deborah's song reappear in the Psalms of David, the reader is reminded once more of the force and permanence of women's history. Mimetic relationship is illustrated by Deborah's earlier prophecy that "the Lord will deliver Sisera into the hands of a woman" when a woman, Jael, after inviting the opposing Sisera into her tent, drives a stake through his head. The scene of Sisera's mother at the window painfully reminds us that for every victor there is a vanquished (Judges 5:28). After Deborah's victory and song, "the land had rest forty years." Forty years, of course, is how long Moses stayed with his wife before the return to Egypt, how long the children of Israel wandered in the desert.

Deborah definitely sets a standard. Is there anyone who wouldn't want a woman for commander-in-chief if it meant the land would have rest for forty years? As a spiritual guide to life, the Bible certainly does not relegate women to proscribed positions.

Getting What You Ask For

The story of Jephthah's daughter is certainly a rough place. It is one of those biblical accounts people point to when they say the Bible is anti-woman. Jephthah has an interesting background. The Bible says that he is the son of a prostitute and Gilead. The other sons of Gilead drive him out, saying he is the son of an outsider. But some time later the brothers come back to him and ask him to lead them in a fight with the Ammonites. He does so on the condition that if the Lord delivers the Ammonites to him then he will become commander over them all. "Then the spirit of the Lord came upon Jephthah. He marched across many territories and came to the Ammonites and made the following vow to the Lord: 'If you de-liver the Ammonites into my hands, then whoever comes out of the door of my house to meet me on my safe return shall be the Lord's and shall be offered by me as a burnt offering'" (Judges 11:29–31 TNK).

Among other things, the story warns one to be careful about what is asked for and what is promised. The grim result is that when Jephthah gets what he asks for, it is his only daughter, his only child, who comes from his house, forcing him to change his mind or bring her to sacrifice. He doesn't change his mind. Unlike Abraham, his concept of God is still locked into an outdated concept of Deity as rigid and requiring sacrifice.

The daughter is unnamed. She acquiesces to her father's vow and asks only that she be allowed to spend two months with her female companions to go to the mountains—"as she had not known man." The idea apparently is not only that she will bear no seed, but also that Jephthah's biological line dies as a result of his own rash vow. However there is much more to the story and to the

Book of Judges. Mieke Bal, cultural theorist, professor of literature, and author of *Death and Dissymmetry: The Politics of Coherence in the Book of Judges*, brilliantly addresses sexuality, powerlessness, and death in Judges. Anyone interested in the intricate nuances, repeated themes, Hebrew meanings, and readings of the book must consult Bal's classic text.

The tale of the unnamed daughter whose father makes an ill-considered vow is not a very comforting story; it is certainly a warning to make no foolish vows, certainly a case of a woman and woman's seed being attacked before bearing fruit. The final verse of the chapter, in which the daughter companions with other women and joins in a ritual memorializing women, makes a further point. It simply illustrates not only women's need for each other, but also the protection such company affords. "And it was a custom in Israel, That the daughters of Israel went yearly to lament the daughter of Jephthah the Gildeadite for four days in a year" (Judges 11:40).

Again there is the rather mysterious *four days*, as in the *fourth day* of spiritual Creation. The lament may well be for the attack on womanhood in the name of an outdated sense of what the biblical Being requires.

In a "time when every man does that which is right in his own eyes" (Judges 17:6), the solidarity among and between women is plain. There is no reader who does not know the feeling these women must have had. There is room here for speculation that the story says all death is unfair—highlighted as the account is by the daughter's innocence.

Alcohol and the Fetus and Samson

In Judges 13, Samson's mother is a woman first identified not by her given name but by her relation to men as wife, woman, mother. Her story is, in some ways, both specific and generic. The story of Samson's mother includes words, phrases, and actions found in the previous stories of Sarah, Abraham, Isaac, Rebekah, Rachel, Jacob,

Moses, and Mary to come. And it twice includes a warning from an angel of God to pregnant women that now, thousands of years later, is found in public service messages and on liquor bottles: "Now be careful not to drink wine or strong drink" (Judges 13:4, 14). The knowledge that alcohol can damage the fetus has been with the culture since the time of Samson's mother.

The story also includes another instance of God controlling reproduction and God appearing first to a woman rather than a man, and a woman offering logical and correct advice to a distraught man. Samson's own story in Judges 13–16 can easily be read as that of a spoiled, demanding, promiscuous, foolish, blind-to-all-but-himself man. He marries, and his wife coaxes an answer to a riddle from him. He sleeps with a whore. He falls in love with Delilah, and she too coaxes an answer from him that becomes his downfall and the downfall of the temple. But there is no biblical judgment on whether he is good or bad. Mieke Bal suggests the story is counterpoint to that of Jephthah. It is the case that the major accounts of Judges involve women and men in relationships fraught with change and that sexual relationships are often at the center of every one of the stories.

The story of Samson is the stuff not only of opera but also of novels. Replete with wordplay in Hebrew, the story illustrates the enduring nature of an old story that is known at least in sketch form even today—the long hair, the blinded eyes, the pulling down of the temple. In particular, the words of Delilah to Samson may sound familiar to many modern readers. It's safe to say that some woman somewhere is asking her man the same question now even as Delilah did then: "How can you say, 'I love you,' when you won't confide in me?" (Judges 16:15 NIV).

Ending as the Beginning

Toward the end of Judges is a story that echoes the dismembering of Adonibezek in the opening of the book. There is a cutting up and scattering abroad. As one looks at this tale, one sees recurrent biblical words and symbols. Beginning again with "no king in Israel" (Judges 19:1–2), this time there is reference to a concubine who played whore. This reference in Judges 19:1–2—as well as references to varying days on which activity takes place and to *straw* and *room to lodge in*—previously had placed such words in the realm of biblical faithfulness and hospitality as well as in the domain of politics.

In this horrible story (if taken literally), a man offers—as a substitute for a man who is his guest—his daughter (as did Lot) and wife-concubine to the sons of Belial. His guest is a man whom no one else would take in; he has plenty of food and straw and is on the way from Bethlehem to Ephraim and to the House of the Lord. There may be something sacred about that information, but if so it is only implied. And the host "took his concubine, and brought her forth unto them; and they knew her, and abused her all the night until the morning: and when the day began to spring, they let her go" (Judges 19:25).

There is no report of how the woman felt. If emotions enter into this part of the biblical account, they are the reader's and not in the text. The text forces readers to react and to reflect on their own feelings and thoughts. But there are two other things readers might note about this scene. One, obviously, is that the female is seemingly valueless. The other is that the father, husband, or lover divides the abused, dead woman at his door into twelve parts— twelve like the tribes of Israel and later the twelve disciples—and sends these to all parts of Israel.

Certainly the female body is being spread throughout Israel. The biblical comment on this story is

And it was so, that all that saw it said, There was no such deed done nor seen from the day that the children of Israel came up out of the land of Egypt unto this day: consider of it, take advice and speak your minds. (Judges 19:30)

Paradox

The last story in the Book of Judges is about the capture of four hundred nameless young virgins from Shiloh. In typical biblical paradox, this prefaces a series of stories that we will look at through the next several chapters of the Bible that laud, praise, celebrate, and honor specific, named, independent women.

Looking closely at Judges we see that the rough places are descriptive, horrendous, allegorical, and instructive. Equally, they are warnings, advice, figurations, and prefigurations as plain as the advice to not cross the street against the light nor touch a hot stove with your bare hand. Beware of both women and men.

Plain Places

What if we are the first full generation of men and women who say, once and for all, that the biblical God loves women as Her full idea, cherishes women, understands women, and helps women wherever they are?

We can start this process by remembering what the biblical God, the Spirit of God, The Breasted One, The Existing One, the Shield who bears the people on eagle's wings has done for women so far in just six books of the Bible:

- Created women as the highest idea of generic man
- Illustrated the dangers of domination of women
- Showed that there are no limits to conception
- Sent angels to powerless, fearful women
- Appeared to women's eyes
- Saved women's children
- Gave women husbands who love them
- Provided homes for independent women

- Protected women
- Healed women of physical ills
- Approved women's strength and leadership abilities
- Appointed women as leaders
- Made women rulers over their own bodies and minds
- Gave women occasion to sing and dance
- Said women work equally with men
- Anointed women to carry the message of God to all
- Exempted women from criticism on sexual, domestic, and political actions

These are simply the most obvious things.

What woman—aware, inspired by the Spirit of God and the Creation of us all as the apex of that Creation in an ordered universe (and a dimension beyond even the universe)—would want a limited, stultifying life of suffering and punishment?

Who would be Eve?

7

The Woman Alone

So the woman went her way, and did eat, and her countenance
was no more sad.

—1 Samuel 18

We no longer have to ask if it is the widow, the orphan, the
powerless woman who carries the story of the Spirit of God to earth.
Being a woman alone is not a dead-end street but an open way to
happiness, fulfillment, and self-esteem. Or so says the Bible.

Taking a look at the women in the Book of Ruth and on into
the First Book of Samuel, we see that not only does God provide
for the woman alone, but that without seemingly powerless women
there would be no story of God's provision for earth. No completeness and no happy ending.

Faithful or Smart?

The familiar line, "whither thou goest, I will go; and where thou
lodgest I will lodge: thy people shall be my people, and thy God my
God" (Ruth 1:16) is Ruth's. Many have thought that a woman says
that to a man, but in fact Ruth says it to her mother-in-law, Naomi.
These phrases have been associated with the marriage ceremony
and, in the past, have often been used to relegate both Ruth and
Naomi to nonthreatening, stereotypical roles by casting them as
devoted daughter-in-law and helpless widowed mother-in-law.

No, Ruth and Naomi are not one-dimensional figures. They are
smart women making smart choices. They may seem powerless at
first blush, but they are protected, guided, nurtured, elevated as they

know themselves while they clearly, oh so clearly, assess their options in a sexist world. They represent the superseding of a hopeless condition by spiritual sense. They illustrate a narrative of spiritual power for women.

Bitter and Sweet

The Book of Ruth is a slim volume. In just four chapters it tells the story of how women alone make it in the world and how David—slayer of Goliath, psalmist, and king of Israel—came to earth. These four chapters are breathtaking in their simplicity and allusion. Sections like this are what make the Bible the Book it is—inspiration, not mere information.

In these four chapters the women are widowed; made outcasts in the land; return to Naomi's original home; find housing, employment, and the protection of the most powerful man in the community; and ensure an heir to be remembered forever. Not bad work for two women in any time or place.

Start reading Ruth and you will see again that the story starts out naming men and then, in a few verses, switches to women, and things actually start happening. Naomi is the central figure. Her husband and two sons have died, leaving two daughters-in-law from Moab, where Naomi had moved with her husband.

> Then she arose with her daughters-in-law, that she might
> return from the country of Moab: for she had heard in the
> country of Moab how that the Lord had visited his people
> in giving them bread. (Ruth 1:6)

It was in Moab that Moses died. Naomi was from Bethlehem, to which she wants to return. As Abraham did, Naomi gets up and goes. But Abraham did not move until he heard a direct order from God. Naomi acts too on something she has heard—God is visiting the people, as God visited Sarah.

Few things in the Bible are more glorious to any woman today than the sight of women finding their own way against all odds.

Orpah, one daughter-in-law, finds hers when she returns to her people; Ruth and Naomi find theirs when they return to Bethlehem in the barley harvest. The signification is clear. In pastoral times, where would you be but at home in the midst of plenty? Harvest time is not just a season of the year but symbolic of abundance.

Naomi is a marvelous character. She reenters Bethlehem— meaning "house of bread"—after years of exile in Moab with husband and sons. In *The Complete Jewish Bible* translation, she says, "Call me not Naomi, call me Mara: for Shaddai has made my lot very bitter" (Ruth 1:20). This is a specific allusion known to all of the listening townspeople of those who had left Egypt with Miriam, Moses, and Aaron and found bitter (Marah) waters after crossing the Red Sea. Here is a woman not afraid to call attention to her problems. Many things can be learned from Naomi. She did have faith that the Almighty—The Breasted One—was providing. But still she let everyone know that her life was not uneventful.

You may feel the same way. You may feel the Almighty is caring for you but that you have also gotten the short end of the stick. Through this ebbing and flowing stage of consciousness, Naomi is cared for. Ruth asks permission to go to the field "and glean ears of corn after him in whose sight I shall find grace" (Ruth 2:2). The field belongs to Boaz, who by Hebrew law is in the line of men who owe the women protection.

Naomi is a fascinating mother-in-law, not only generous and dramatic, but prescient: when Ruth asks her what to do about Boaz, Naomi tells her that he is a redeeming kinsman and that "[t]he man will not be in rest, until he have finished the thing this day" (Ruth 3:18).

Wings in the Wilderness

Ruth, like Sarah and Abraham, has left her family. And she too is rewarded. "May you have a full recompense from the Lord, the God of Israel, under whose wings you have sought refuge," says Boaz to Ruth when he finds her working in the field. Those wings again, as in Exodus, bringing the children of Israel—and in this case, a daughter of Moab—under the protection of the nurturing Mother-hood of God. When Boaz declares to the townspeople that he will marry Ruth, in Eugene H. Peterson's translation, *The Message* (2002), the people respond, "May God make this woman who is coming into your household like Rachel and Leah, the two women who built the family of Israel" (Ruth 4:11).

Each verse of this story might well be examined by women who feel alienated, adrift, hungry, unloved, as well as by women and men who think they are planning their own futures. Take a look at the barley harvest. It meets the human need. Using the concordance to look up *fruit* and *harvest* in the Bible may also lead to a sense of ful-fillment. We can learn how Shaddai provides in our own individual manner.

Building the House of Israel

As inspiration, Ruth and Naomi live forever in poetry and history. They are also the great-grandmother and great-great-grandmother of David, the psalmist, unifier of Israel, lover of many women, and a central figure in the line of prophecy. Ruth, David's great-grandmother, is a Moabitess, a descendent of Lot and his daughter. Boaz, who will marry Ruth and father her child, is a descendant of Tamar (who played the harlot to ensure her rights in the face of her forgetful father-in-law, Judah). The initiative of these women—Lot's daughters on the female side and Tamar on the male side—bring the biological David into the world. And it is David who unifies Israel by accepting the foreigners and the strangers. When we remember that his great-grandmother was a foreigner and stranger in Bethlehem and we remember how many of us have learned from our ancestors, we see again the importance of women in shaping the course of history.

Follow the Women

Ruth's and Hannah's stories are not consecutive in the Hebrew Bible as they are in the King James Version. Either way, one may well want to read on from the Book of Ruth without interruption to the First Book of Samuel and to Hannah—whose story, like Ruth's, begins with a man who fades into the landscape of the desires and needs of women. There is no question that in the chapters the Bible is unfolding its story of Creation through women.

Knowing and Desire

Hannah is a key biblical figure. Not only does she share with Rachel the provocations of another wife, not only is she the most beloved, but she establishes silent prayer by defending it to the priest (1 Samuel 1:2–18). Hannah is the beloved, though barren, wife of a man named Elkanah. Certainly it is not because she is loved, or the fact that she envies and is provoked by the other wife who does have children, that her name lives today as one of the seven women prophets of Israel. She lives on because of how she prayed; her specificity; her sense of certainty about her own individual relationship, rights, and access to the Eternal Creator; and her song.

Take note of Hannah's prayer from verse 11 of the first chapter of 1 Samuel. Note the same bitterness that the women encountered after the parting of the seas, the same bitterness Naomi spoke of earlier. Follow along with Hannah and note how specific she is.

> And she vowed a vow, and said, O Lord of Hosts (Existing One of the Whole Creation), If you will look upon the affliction of your handmaid, and remember me, and not forget me, but will give unto your handmaid a man child, then I will give him unto the Lord all the days of his life, and no razor shall touch his head. (1 Samuel 1:11)

Translators Miss the Mark?

The King James and Hebrew translations say that Hannah prayed to the "Lord God of hosts." But the Hebrew words for *Lord God* and *hosts* are defined as "Existing One for Lord," and *hosts* is also defined as "whole creation." So although the male translators chose Lord God of hosts, it could just as well be that Hannah is making a vow to The Existing One of the Whole Creation—just as today in our private prayers we choose the words we use to address God.

Hannah is seen praying by Eli, the priest. He sees not into her heart. Only that her lips move. He says: "How long will you make a drunken spectacle of yourself? Sober up!" (1 Samuel 1:14 TNK).

Then Hannah contradicts the priest. The reader will note that when Hannah is misrepresented by the priest—and talks back to him—she is not censured, ostracized, or cast out of organized religion. The reader will also note that the biblical designation for men—"my lord"—is the same as the translators have used for God, even if there are alternative Hebrew definitions or meanings for the words for God. Small wonder that God and men seem one and the same in many places in the Bible, or that man associates with God and women are perceived as not male, not God or Godlike.

Hannah responds:

> Oh no, my lord! I am a very unhappy woman. I have drunk no wine or other strong drink, but I have been pouring my heart out to the Lord. (1 Samuel 1:15 TNK)

The priest gives up. After the fact, he gives Hannah a priestly blessing.

> So the woman went her way, and did eat, and her countenance was no more sad. (1 Samuel 1:18)

Hannah and her husband Elkanah worship before The Existing One of the Whole Creation and return home, and "Elkanah knew Hannah, his wife; and the Lord remembered her" (1 Samuel 1:19).

Here is one of the countless places in the Bible in which the text illustrates the side-by-side creations of Genesis, chapters 1 and 2. Elkanah, like Adam, knew his wife. But the Lord remembered Hannah—as God remembered Noah, as Rachel was remembered. Hannah conceives as easily and as surely as two and two is four. It is almost a mathematical equation—*knowing and remembering*. It is a spiritual agreement. Hannah's first child, Samuel, will anoint David, great-grandson of Ruth, great-great-grandson of Naomi, as king of Israel. The line of women is unmistakable, not just biologically but in the anointing, prophesying, praying, acting, being, doing, living with the Creative Spirit of the Bible.

God, the Territory

Peterson, in *The Message*, makes an interesting note in his introduction to 1–2 Samuel: "Four lives dominate the two-volume narrative: Hannah, Samuel, Saul and David. Not one of them can be accounted for in terms of cultural conditions or psychological dynamics. God is the country in which they live" (p. 457).

Hannah had prayed silently for this child Samuel, and after his birth she prays aloud. Her prayer is not a sweet "thank you" but, as we read in 1 Samuel 2:1–10:

My heart rejoices in the Lord [The Existing One]
In the Lord my horn is lifted high.
My mouth boasts over my enemies
For I delight in your deliverance.

There is no one holy like the Lord:
there is no one besides you;
there is no Rock like our God.

Read on to a sampling of lines in which Hannah says:

The bows of the warriors are broken,
But those who stumbled are armed with strength
She who was barren has borne seven children,
But she who has had many sons pines away
The Lord brings death and makes alive
For the foundations of the earth are the Lord's
Those who oppose the Lord will be shattered
The Lord will judge the ends of the earth
And exalt the horn of his anointed

This is not tame stuff. Nor is it bragging. It is prophecy spilling out of the mouth of a biblical mother. Mary repeats part of Hannah's song when she receives the angelic message that she will bear a child through The Existing One alone. Women through the ages, biblical and otherwise, are connected to each other, live and move and have their being in God as well as in each other's hopes and aspirations.

Diplomacy Interrupts War

The Bible says that your own prophetic ability can get you out of a bad marriage. In less than two weeks, Abigail, a lovely but unknown woman of great wisdom married to a foolish drunk, becomes a prophet newly married to a gracious, passionate, warrior poet—the Lord's anointed and the king of Israel.

Although we hear most often about David and Bathsheba or about David and Saul's daughter, Michal, nevertheless the story of David and women is at its romantic high point with Abigail—neither a seducer nor the seduced nor the daughter of a powerful man. Abigail is another of the seven woman prophets of Israel, a most political woman living a political life, and by almost any definition one of the smartest.

In his book *The Life of David*, the poet Robert Pinsky says about the story of David: "With its emphasis on competition and succession, loyalty and rivalry among men and between sons and fathers, it seems a male story, in the primal way of ironbound tradition; yet women play powerful roles. Michal, Abigail, Bathsheba, make decisions that determine outcomes" (2005, p. 7).

We know at least a sketch of David's life. He is the youngest, the clever son who is anointed by Samuel. Samuel has been raised in the Temple as per his mother's vow and is now the prophet of Israel. David slays Goliath, "the uncircumcised Philistine giant who defies the armies of the Living God"; he has been in the house of Saul, whom the people have made king, singing psalms to calm Saul. He has come in triumph after his victory over Goliath, simply accomplished with five smooth stones, and Saul gives him his second daughter, Michal, as wife. Both Pinsky and Robert Alter, in his David translation and commentary *The David Story* (1999), explicate the life of this complicated biblical hero in depth; those books should be read for more understanding of David.

Our concern here is the women in David's life, particularly Abigail, as she seems the most interesting and multifaceted of them all and appears more fully in the text than David's other wives.

David's victory over Goliath is past. David is already married to Michal, has survived Saul's jealousy and repeated attacks, and has taken refuge for a time in Ramah with Hannah's son, the prophet Samuel. Now, just after Samuel's death, David is grieving.

> David arose, and went down to the wilderness of Paran.
> And there was a man in Maon, whose possession were in
> Carmel; and the man was very great, and he had three
> thousand sheep, and a thousand goats; and he was shearing
> his sheep in Carmel. Now the name of the man was Nabal;
> and the name of his wife Abigail: and she was a woman of
> good understanding, and of a beautiful countenance: but
> the man was churlish and evil in his doings; and he was
> of the house of Caleb. (1 Samuel 25:1–3)

About the Woman

Here again the Bible begins a story about men and then switches to the story of a woman. And again, the story shows that how men and women treat each other has national and international repercussions through time. The story continues as David sends ten of his men over to Carmel to greet Nabal in David's name and to request hospitality. On our trip through the Bible so far we have already seen that hospitality is the number-one prerequisite for entertaining angels and God and, in a more general sense, for making one's way through the wilderness of doubt to hope.

Remember that Abraham exhibits hospitality (Genesis 18) to the three men who announce that Sarah, at ninety, will conceive, and, in one of the 125 biblical references to the word *stranger*, The Existing One says in Exodus 22:21–23: "Thou shalt neither vex a stranger, nor oppress him: for ye were strangers in the land of Egypt. Ye shall not afflict any widow, or fatherless child. If thou afflict them in any wise, and they cry at all unto me, I will surely hear their cry."

It's a mandate.

Yet Nabal refuses hospitality to David's men, saying he's never heard of this David and wonders if perhaps he is just a runaway servant. David—macho to the hilt—girds up his sword at this response and takes four hundred armed men with him in a plan to attack Nabal. Readers will note that four hundred armed warriors is the same number that Jacob was told accompanied his estranged twin, Esau. No loose ends in biblical accounts of men arming themselves to settle personal disputes.

> One of the servants told Nabal's wife Abigail: David sent messengers from the desert to give our master his greetings, but he hurled insults at them. Yet these men were very good to us. They did not mistreat us, and the whole time we were out in the fields near them nothing was missing . . .
>
> Now think it over and see what you can do, because disaster is hanging over our master and his whole household.

He is such a wicked man that no one can talk to him.
(1 Samuel 25:14–15 NIV)

Abigail Takes Action

The men are asking the woman what she thinks should be done; they expect her to take care of things. Abigail is hardly a chattel in a burqa. She doesn't pause for an instant. She doesn't defend her husband. Nor does she run and tell her friends or her mother that she married a horrible man who is disgracing her and might even get her killed. She takes matters into her own hands—immediately.

> Abigail lost no time. She took two hundred loaves of bread, two skins of wine, five dressed sheep, five seahs of roasted grain, a hundred cakes of raisins and two hundred cakes of pressed figs and loaded them on donkeys.
>
> Then she told her servants, "Go on ahead; I'll follow you." But she did not tell her husband Nabal. As she came riding her donkey into a mountain ravine, there were David and his men descending toward her, and she met them.
> (1 Samuel 25:18–20 NIV)

Not only does this look like a generous picnic feast, not only does Abigail not tell her husband, but she has quite clearly moved into the land of spiritual territory and prophecy. "I'll follow you," is translated by the King James Version as "behold, I come after you," and is reminiscent of what John the Baptist will say later. Riding on a donkey is not just a method of transportation in Abigail's times. The animal represents an announcement of protection or things to come. Among other donkey riders, Moses led Zipporah and their children into Egypt, later Joseph will lead Mary and her child on the way to Egypt, and Jesus rides a donkey as palms are thrown before him prior to his crucifixion.

Abigail is on her way to intercept a furious David—a David boiling over with self-righteous male indignation. The Hebrew translation is "Now David had been saying, 'It was all for nothing that I protected that fellow's possessions in the wilderness, and that nothing he owned is missing. He has paid me back evil for good. May God do thus and more to the enemies of David if, by the light of morning, I leave a single male of his [literally: anyone who pees against a wall].'" The King James has this as "any that pisseth against the wall" (1 Samuel 25:21–22 NIV).

That's about as macho as it gets.

Ambassador for Peace

When Abigail sees David, she gets off the donkey and falls to the ground in front of his feet. Some, over the years, have read this act as groveling or obsequious, others as grace and truth more powerful than any military might. Either way, it is the opening of a clever piece of politics and actions in the line of prophecy. Here is what she says in Peterson's translation, *The Message*: "My master, let me take the blame! Let me speak to you. Listen to what I have to say. Don't dwell on what that brute Nabal did. He acts out the meaning of his name: Nabal, Fool. Foolishness oozes from him" (1 Samuel 25:25).

Whether we think Abigail has just trashed her husband, told the truth about him, or ended slaughter and war before it started — and whether we think that what Abigail says next makes her a flatterer or a model of diplomacy and candidate for ambassador or secretary of state—this passage forces us to examine our beliefs about a woman's response to a dangerous situation.

Bundle of Life

Turning to a tight and intricate reference to David and God, she prophecies. She says only God is more powerful than David, even though she is quite powerful as she interrupts David on his way to murder her husband.

She continues,

Forgive my presumption! But God is at work in my master, developing a rule solid and dependable. My master fights God's battles! As long as you live no evil will stick to you.
If anyone stands in your way,
If anyone tries to get you out of the way,
Know this: Your God-honored life is tightly bound
In the bundle of God-protected life;
But the lives of your enemies will be hurled aside
As a stone is thrown from a sling.

When God completes all the goodness he has promised my master and sets you up as a prince over Israel, my master will not have this dead weight in his heart, the guilt of an avenging murder. (1 Samuel 25:24–31, Peterson)

Most readers have favorite verses in the King James Version, and one favored verse is this: "The soul of my lord shall be bound in the bundle of life with the Lord thy God." That is the same verse that Peterson translates as "Know this: Your God-honored life is tightly bound in the bundle of God-protected life." To see someone bound in the bundle of life is a glimpse of spiritual Creation.

Miriam's song, Deborah's, Hannah's, all carry much wisdom and strength and prophecy. Abigail uses an alert reference to the sling, which David used to slay Goliath—a reference David knows only too well. Learning from Abigail, we might well master the art of pulling out a handy fact to serve our purposes and those of The Existing One. She instructs David to *remember* her. Abigail ties David to Eternal Life, Eternal Life to David, and herself to both. She too "is bound in the bundle of life."

David Yields

David's response makes it easy to see why so many women loved him.

And David said to Abigail, Blessed be the Lord God of Israel [or Blessed be The Existing One, the true God,

God who prevails] which sent thee this day to meet me: And blessed be thy advice, and blessed be thou, which has kept me this day from coming to shed blood, and from avenging myself with mine own hand. For in this very deed, as the Lord God of Israel liveth, which hath kept me back from hurting thee, except thou hadst hasted and come to meet me, surely there had not been left unto Nabal by the morning light any that pisseth against the wall. (1 Samuel 25:32–34)

Now the man David puts God, not himself, first. David acknowledges that Abigail is acting for God. He puts her advice in the category of the sixth and seventh days of spiritual Creation by calling it blessed. And not only does he think her advice is beyond all human advice, but he specifically acknowledges her actions. Nice to have a man appreciate you the way David appreciates Abigail. He says, "Go up in peace to thine house; see, I have hearkened to thy voice, and have accepted thy person." David accepts not merely Abigail's evidences of hospitality, not merely her words, not only her deeds. He gives the most important acceptance of all: the acceptance of her as a person.

Poetic Justice

The story comes to poetic fulfillment without missing a beat in 1 Samuel: 36–42. Abigail goes home to find Nabal drunk and stuffing himself with food. In the morning when he is sober, Abigail tells him what went on between her and David. At the news, Nabal has a heart attack. Ten days later he dies.

Then David sent word to Abigail, asking her to become his wife.

Not only is there no traditional mourning period here, but they must have had a great time communing, and she must have said "yes," because David sends his servants to her house "to take her to him to wife." She is his third wife.

We are conditioned today to have a respectable mourning period after a spouse's death and to be careful not to marry out of some codependent or psychotic need. Whatever the source of those current concerns, they are not the Bible's at this point.

In yet another example of how women exhibit the leading thought in the biblical path, Abigail washes the feet of David's servants, as the unnamed woman will do later for Jesus, and as Jesus will do for his disciples.

> And Abigail hasted, and arose, and rode upon an ass, with five damsels of hers that went after her; and she went after the messengers of David, and became his wife.

Her story does not end there. She is later captured by enemies of David, is rescued by him, has a child by him; she is yet another biblical woman whose experience is full of adventure.

Women and David

There is no question that the women who come into contact with David have their share of adventure, danger, drama, and triumph. A partial list of women who have encounters with David includes Michal (second wife), Bathsheba (his eighth named wife), Abigail, Abishag (who warmed him in his old age), women like Rizpah (whose sons died in David's reign), two Tamars (his daughter and a granddaughter), Ahinoam (his first wife), and Zerulah, his half-sister.

In David's time, there are also wise women, the witch at Endor, and the women widowed and left fatherless by David's battles as he unified Israel. The list of women influenced and affected by David even after his death (recorded in 1 Kings 2:10) is a long one and interesting too in that it illustrates clearly a variety of women and of female experience.

And the women? How did they influence David? Did David write down all those wonderful Psalms—full of ideas that feed the heart of women starving for spiritual comfort—as they fell from the lips of Abigail, Bathsheba, Michal, or Abishag?

8

Psalms

They that go down to the sea in ships, that do business in great waters; these see the works of the Lord, and his wonders in the deep.

—Psalms 107:23–24

The Psalms refer to spiritual Creation, the crossing of the Red Sea and the Jerusalem Temple. Female experience—all experience—is enriched by the Psalms. Written at different times and under different circumstances, the Psalms are prophetic, personal and impersonal, individual, national, reflective, timely, and, to some, boastful. The Twenty-third Psalm, which begins, "The Lord is my shepherd," and the Ninety-first, "He that dwelleth in the secret place of the most High shall abide under the shadow of the Almighty," are familiar comforts to many. Jesus repeats the prophetic Psalm 22 on the cross (Matthew 27:46).

In some ways, Psalms can be read as an overview of the Bible. Some, like Psalm 22, are referred to later in the Bible. Other Psalms go back into parts of the Bible we have already read. Psalm 106 recaps the story of Moses and the Children of Israel led out of Egypt. Psalm 104 comments on spiritual Creation, as does Psalm 148.

Whether many scribes had a hand in the Psalms, or whether David wrote down some of those attributed to him while in the presence of Abigail, Bathsheba, Michal, Abishag, or any of the women who made his life richer is of less importance than the fact that the reader today can search through them with the knowledge that the author lived a full life, loved women, and speaks out of experience.

My voice shalt thou hear in the morning, O Lord; in the morning will I direct my prayer unto thee, and will look up. (Psalm 5:3)

No one can deny that the King James Version's translation of the Hebrew Psalms is gorgeous. But because anyone not reading the Original Hebrew is reading a translation, it is useful to look at a familiar psalm in several translations to help us identify what version gives us the most inspiration and to see what the translators of the past have done.

The Twenty-third Psalm—which begins, in the King James Version, "The Lord is my shepherd; I shall not want"—reads in the Jewish Publication Society's Tanakh as "The Lord is my shepherd, I lack nothing." Peterson's *The Message* translates the verse rather as "God, my shepherd, I don't need a thing."

But it is interesting to use a concordance to see what is translated or the translation behind the translation. Strong's Concordance uses for the definition of "Jehovah = 'the existing One': the proper name of the one true God, unpronounced except with the vowel pointings of 0136." And, for *shepherd*, the obvious "to pasture, tend, graze or feed" but also "to associate with, be a friend of (meaning probable) (Qal) to associate with (Hithpael) to be companions (Piel) to be a special friend."

As gorgeous or pithy as the translations are, it seems that this could as easily have been translated: "The Existing One is my companion" or "my associate" or even perhaps: "I associate with The Existing One," which seems a bit more gender-neutral, more inclusive than the ubiquitous *Lord* used by the translators to date. But why not use a concordance and find other terminology already extant that broadens the concept of the Deity?

The musician Bobby McFerrin has done that in his translation of the Twenty-third Psalm, which he dedicated to his mother. He begins with the familiar, "The Lord is my shepherd" but continues, "She makes me lie down in green meadows." He continues to the end, interspersing familiar lines of the psalm with uses of the feminine plural, making reference to living in Her house forever.

The Psalms give us a timeless break from the Bible's narrative, and there are few who cannot find some passage that does not inspire and comfort. But in reading them with the sweeping use of "the Lord" for the more nuanced or feminine meanings for God in the Hebrew, we find ourselves subservient to a male God rather than the Creative Spirit that we know God is. Perhaps a substitution of your own word for Lord or The Existing One could bring deeper meaning and immediacy to a reading of the Bible, and of the Psalms.

Some of those verses from the King James version may even have particular resonance for women when read as the women we are today.

O ye sons of men, how long will ye turn my glory into shame? How long will ye love vanity, and seek after leasing? (Psalm 4:2)

I will both lay me down in peace, and sleep; for thou Lord [Existing One] only makest me dwell in safety. (Psalm 4:8)

My voice shalt thou hear in the morning, O Lord; in the morning will I direct my prayer unto thee, and will look up. (Psalm 5:3)

For thou art not a God that hath pleasure in wickedness: neither shall evil dwell with thee. (Psalm 5:4)

Lead me, O Lord, in thy righteousness because of mine enemies; make they way straight before my face. (Psalm 5:8)

Depart from me, all ye workers of iniquity; for the Lord hath heard the voice of my weeping.

The Lord hath heard my supplication; the Lord will receive
my prayer. (Psalm 6:8–9)

Lord, thou hast heard the desire of the humble; thou
wilt prepare their heart, thou wilt cause thine ear to hear:
To judge the fatherless and the oppressed, that the man
of the earth may no more oppress.
(Psalm 10:17–18)

Keep me as the apple of thy eye, hide me under the shadow
of thy wings. (Psalm 17:8)

Hearken, O daughter, and consider, and incline thine ear,
forget also thine own people, and thy father's house; so shall
the King greatly desire thy beauty. . . . The King's daughter
is all glorious within; her clothing is of wrought gold.
(Psalm 45:10–11, 13)

God is in the midst of her; she shall not be moved: God
shall help her and that right early. (Psalm 46:5)

A father of the fatherless, and a judge of the widows, is
God in his holy habitation. God setteth the solitary in
families; he bringeth out those which are bound with
chains; but the rebellious dwell in a dry land. . . .
(Psalm 68:5–6)

Cast me not off in the time of old age: forsake me not when
my strength faileth. Now also when I am old and greyheaded,
O God, forsake me not; until I have shewed thy strength unto
this generation and thy power to every one that is to come.
(Psalm 71:9, 18)

He healeth the broken in heart, and bindeth up their wounds.
(Psalm 147:3)

Creation: Genesis

When I consider thy heavens, the work of thy fingers,
the moon and the stars, which thou hast ordained;
What is man, that thou art mindful of him? and the
son of man, that thou visitest him?
For thou hast made him a little lower than the angels,
and hast crowned him with glory and honour.
Thou madest him to have dominion over the works
of thy hands; thou hast put all things under his feet:
All sheep and oxen, yea, and the beasts of the field;
The fowl of the air, and the fish of the sea, and
whatsoever passeth through the paths of the seas.
O Lord our Lord, how excellent is thy name in all
the earth! (Psalm 8)

The heavens declare the glory of God; and the firmament
sheweth his handiwork. (Psalm 19:1)

He trusted on the Lord that he would deliver him: let him
deliver him, seeing he delighted in him.
But thou art he that took me out of the womb: thou
didst make me hope when I was upon my mother's breasts.
(Psalm 22:8–9)

Lord, thou hast been our dwelling place in all generations.
Before the mountains were brought forth, or ever thou
hadst formed the earth and the world, even from everlasting
to everlasting, thou art God. (Psalm 90:1–2)

Who coverest thyself with light as with a garment: who
stretchest out the heavens like a curtain:
Who layeth the beams of his chambers in the waters:
who maketh the clouds his chariot: who walketh upon the
wings of the wind:

Who maketh his angels spirits; his ministers a flaming fire:

Who laid the foundations of the earth, that it should not be removed for ever.

Thou coveredst it with the deep as with a garment: the waters stood above the mountains. . . .

O Lord, how manifold are thy works! in wisdom hast thou made them all: the earth is full of thy riches.

So is this great and wide sea, wherein are things creeping innumerable, both small and great beasts.

There go the ships: there is that leviathan, whom thou hast made to play therein. These wait all upon thee; that thou mayest give them their meat in due season. That thou givest them they gather: thou openest thine hand, they are filled with good. (Psalm 104:2–6, 24–28)

Whither shall I go from thy spirit? or whither shall I flee from thy presence?

If I ascend up into heaven, thou art there: if I make my bed in hell, behold, thou art there.

If I take the wings of the morning, and dwell in the uttermost parts of the sea;

Even there shall thy hand lead me, and thy right hand shall hold me. (Psalm 139:7–10)

All of Psalm 148:

Praise ye the Lord. Praise ye the Lord from the heavens: praise him in the heights.

Praise ye him, all his angels: praise ye him, all his hosts.

Praise ye him, sun and moon: praise him, all ye stars of light.

Praise him, ye heavens of heavens, and ye waters that be above the heavens.

Let them praise the name of the Lord: for he commanded, and they were created. (Psalm 148:1–5)

9

Kings, Queens, Widows, Prophets

And when the queen of Sheba heard of the fame of Solomon concerning the name of the Lord, she came to prove him with hard questions.

—1 Kings 10:1

The Queen of Sheba makes an international diplomatic mission to Solomon, David's son by Bathsheba. The Queen of Sheba appears in a mere thirteen biblical verses, but volumes of speculation and commentary have been written about her. The story of Solomon and Sheba is one that transcends time and culture and evidences an equal exchange between reigning monarchs. But, as Jacob Lassner points out in his book, *Demonizing the Queen of Sheba: Boundaries of Gender and Culture in Postbiblical Judaism and Medieval Islam* (1993), male commentators through the ages have turned her into a demonic force seeking to dissolve gender boundaries.

It's quite a leap, but not an unusual one. Male commentators on the women of the Bible have most often interpreted those women as mother or harlot—or through the lens of their own view of women as not men but as "other."

After the death of his father, Solomon's first act as king is to marry Pharaoh's daughter. Then he asks The Existing One for an "understanding heart," saying that he is but a little child—though before his life and reign is over he will have seven hundred wives and three hundred concubines. Perhaps one of the best-known stories concerning Solomon is this:

Then came there two women, that were harlots, unto the king, and stood before him.

And the one woman said, O my lord, I and this woman dwell in one house; and I was delivered of a child with her in the house.

And it came to pass the third day after that I was delivered, that this woman was delivered also: and we were together; there was no stranger with us in the house, save we two in the house. And this woman's child died in the night; because she overlaid it. And she arose at midnight, and took my son from beside me, while thine handmaid slept, and laid it in her bosom, and laid her dead child in my bosom. And when I rose in the morning to give my child suck, behold, it was dead: but when I had considered it in the morning, behold, it was not my son, which I did bear. And the other woman said, Nay; but the living is my son, and the dead is thy son. And this said, No; but the dead is thy son, and the living is my son. Thus they spake before the king. (1 Kings 3:16–22)

Solomon's solution is widely known. He says to split the baby in half—but the actual birth mother says to let him live and let the other mother have him, and Solomon determines her desire to see the child live as the sign of true motherhood.

Read without gender bias, the story of the Queen of Sheba and Solomon is one of a series of diplomatic missions by a head of state to a man considered the wisest in the known world.

And she came to Jerusalem with a very great train, with camels that bare spices, and very much gold, and precious stones: and when she was come to Solomon, she communed with him of all that was in her heart.

And Solomon told her all her questions: there was not any thing hid from the king, which he told her not. And she said to the king, It was a true report that I heard in mine own land of thy acts and of thy wisdom. Howbeit I believed not the words, until I came, and mine eyes had seen it: and, behold, the half was not told me: thy wisdom and prosperity exceedeth the fame which I heard.

Happy are thy men, happy are these thy servants, which stand continually before thee, and that hear thy wisdom. (1 Kings 10:2–9)

And—the biblical point—she honors the God of Israel.

Blessed be the Lord thy God, which delighted in thee, to set thee on the throne of Israel: because the Lord loved Israel for ever, therefore made he thee king, to do judgment and justice. And she gave the king one hundred and twenty talents of gold, and of spices very great store, and precious stones: there came no more such abundance of spices as these which the queen of Sheba gave to king Solomon. (1 Kings 10:9–10)

The following translation from the King James Version has led to speculation by some commentators:

And king Solomon gave unto the queen of Sheba all her desire, whatsoever she asked, beside that which Solomon gave her of his royal bounty. So she turned and went to her own country, she and her servants.

Just what was it that she desired? some have asked. Later commentators insisted that there was a sexual relationship—Solomon besting the Queen. In *The Message*, Eugene Peterson, instead of translating "so she turned," rather deftly handles the phrase with this summation: "Satisfied, she returned home with her train of servants."

Right Man, Right Time

What if the Biblical God sends you the right man at the right time? Would you take him in?

Elijah is a case study of the appearance in your life of the right man at the right time. No journey through biblical consciousness is complete without visiting with Elijah. According to the Gospel Scriptures, both Moses and Jesus talk with Elijah on a "high mountain" (Matthew 17:1–13, Luke 9:28–36, Mark 9:2–13).

Both as an individual and as a representative of key themes, Elijah is the archetypal male prophet of the Hebrew Bible. And no one much likes him. Elijah is the prototype for Jesus' well-known statement, delivered while preaching in his own hometown synagogue: "No prophet is accepted in his own country" (Luke 4:24).

Elijah's prophetic ministry is described in part in 1 Kings. Times are terrible for the prophets. Where to go? To a woman, of course.

And the word of the Lord came unto him, saying,
Arise, get thee to Zarephath, which belongeth to Zidon, and dwell there: behold, I have commanded a widow woman there to sustain thee.
So he arose and went to Zarephath. And when he came to the gate of the city, behold, the widow woman was there gathering of sticks: and he called to her, and said, Fetch me, I pray thee, a little water in a vessel, that I may drink.
(1 Kings 17:8–10)

The woman could have told him to get it himself, but she complies. Verse 11 continues, "As she was going to get it, he called, 'And bring me, I pray thee, a morsel of bread in thy hand.'"

Some might think this adds insult to injury; others, that biblical woman is only there to serve men—but we have already seen this is not the case; in fact, as we'll see in this story, the reverse is true. Elijah will serve her well, and The Existing One provides for both male and female. The story of Elijah and the widow woman is a commentary on that first chapter of Genesis—spiritual Creation.

At the request for bread, the woman tells Elijah that she has none. All she has is a handful of flour in a barrel and a little oil in a container. What she is doing—when stopped by Elijah—is gathering sticks for the last scrap of a meal for her son and herself. If, as the text has said, The Existing One has commanded this widow to sustain Elijah, she hasn't heard about it. She is at the end of her rope and ready to die. She can't see beyond the amount of food that she has in the house.

What is it that Elijah says to her?

Fear not. . . . (17:13)

Here again is the injunction to woman to "Fear not." As was true with Hagar by the unseen spring of water, when faced with any complexity, denial, or need, the first biblical command is to fear not. The second is to be hospitable. Elijah reminds her to entertain the stranger. He tells her to go home and make a small bread for him, and then some for her and her son. "For thus saith the Lord God of Israel, The barrel of meal shall not waste, neither shall the cruse of oil fail, until the day that the Lord sendeth rain upon the earth" (1 Kings 17:14).

Oil is a symbol of anointing and prophecy that appears throughout the Bible; a look at the concordance will point to those references. But there is more in this meeting of the powerless, starving woman and the unhappy, homeless male prophet—more even than the jug of oil that never fails.

The Worst Thing

The worst thing that can happen to any mother happens.

And it came to pass after these things, that the son of the woman, the mistress of the house, fell sick; and his sickness was so sore, that there was no breath left in him. And she said unto Elijah, What have I to do with thee, O thou man of God? Art thou come unto me to call my sin to remembrance, and to slay my son? (1 Kings 17:17–18)

The Best Thing

And the best thing that can happen to any mother in that situation happens.

> And he said unto her, Give me thy son. And he took him out of her bosom, and carried him up into a loft, where he abode, and laid him upon his own bed.
>
> And he cried unto the Lord, and said, O Lord my God, hast thou also brought evil upon the widow with whom I sojourn, by slaying her son?
>
> And he stretched himself upon the child three times, and cried unto the Lord, and said, O Lord my God, I pray thee, let this child's soul come into him again.
>
> And the Lord heard the voice of Elijah; and the soul of the child came into him again, and he revived. And Elijah took the child, and brought him down out of the chamber into the house, and delivered him unto his mother: and Elijah said, See, thy son liveth. And the woman said to Elijah, Now by this I know that thou art a man of God, and that the word of the Lord in thy mouth is truth. (1 Kings 17:19–24)

It takes a woman, a widow, to recognize Elijah's truth. A seemingly powerless woman sustains him in his mission. That theme—the powerless woman recognizing Spirit—is repeated throughout the Bible. The widow woman is another in the long, long chain of biblical women who recognize, affirm, and set the seal on the activities of the *ruah Elohim*.

Jezebel

It is also a woman, Queen Jezebel—making her first appearance in 1 Kings 16:31—who is the strongest enemy of Elijah. Jezebel is the opposite of the biblical women we have met so far. She has most of The Existing One's prophets killed. Elijah challenges Jezebel's God, Baal, in a contest over who and what is *All*. Jezebel's name means "Baal exists," according to the Hebrew Lexicon to the Bible (some biblical concordances say it means "unchaste"). Baal worship claims to control fertility and water. Yet the prophets of Baal—who came with Jezebel from her native country to Israel when she married Ahab, the king of the ten northern tribes of Israel—cannot make it rain, no matter what. But water is Spirit's Word—an essential element of spiritual Creation. The *ruah Elohim* has moved on the face of the waters and organized one unfolding Creation. There is one biblical Creator—monotheism is the Bible's calling card. There is no question that there will be a demonstration of the power of the God of the Bible over worshippers of Baal. Elijah calls on The Existing One of Israel, and then he slays Jezebel's prophets with the sword. The rain comes (1 Kings 18:20–46).

From her ivory-towered palace, Jezebel calls out for the death of Elijah within twenty-four hours. He goes where the prophets and Hagar and the children of Israel go, to the wilderness—to Horeb, in this case, where Moses and God spoke and where Moses received the Commandments. There Elijah hears the Voice of God, "not in the wind . . . not in the earthquake . . . not in the fire . . ." but in a "still small voice," a gentle whisper (1 Kings 19:11–12).

Jezebel, a regular breaker of Commandments if ever there was one, demands for her husband that which is not theirs—a neighbor's land. Writing letters in her husband's name, coveting her neighbor's property, she has the owner and heirs to the property stoned to death. The Voice of God tells Elijah that Jezebel will be eaten by dogs. And she is. But not before her husband dies from wounds in battle, her two sons are murdered, and, still unrepentant, she paints her face, fixes her hair, and looked out a window to await and torment the army leader come to kill her. Jezebel's own eunuchs push her out the window (2 Kings 9:30–33). Jezebel has been condemned not for her sexuality, but for ignoring the mandate of hospitality. She has violated the law of kindness to strangers and made the fatal mistake of attacking a messenger of God. We will run into her name again in the Book of Revelation.

Here, There, and Everywhere

As one might expect from the Bible, the prophet Elijah is sustained in the wilderness by an angel of the Lord. Appearances on earth, in the cloud, and who knows where else are the signs of Elijah. He reflects that dominion given male and female on the sixth day of spiritual Creation. His many encounters with women—and theirs with him—are central to his activity. When we read about him, we see that he is here, there, and everywhere, ready to find you or your nation in the most desperate moments.

Elijah takes consciousness into another dimension. He doesn't die; he rises above the earth on a chariot of fire. Elijah is outside chronological time. In the Gospel of Mark to come, Elijah (Elias in the translation from the Greek of the New Testament) is in another example of simultaneous time:

> And after six days Jesus taketh Peter, James, and John his brother, and bringeth them up into an high mountain apart.
>
> And was transfigured before them: and his face did shine as the sun, and his raiment was white as the light. And, behold, there appeared unto them Moses and Elias talking with him.
>
> Then answered Peter, and said unto Jesus, Lord, it is good for us to be here: if thou wilt, let us mark here three tabernacles; one for thee, and one for Moses, and one for Elias. (Mark 9:2–5)

The final biblical note on Elijah is in James 5:17: Elias was a man subject to passions, as we are.

The Book of Prophets

Subject to passions, too, are Amos, Daniel, Ezekiel, Ezra, Habakkuk, Haggai, Hosea, Isaiah, Jeremiah, Job, Joel, Jonah, Joshua, Malachi, Micah, Nahum, Nehemiah, Obadiah, Samuel, Zechariah, and Zephaniah. The Books of the Bible named for these men show them to be of different temperaments, different styles. These men rant and rave and see visions. These men share their dreams and visions with us, and we learn much from their observations and prophecies about women and nations, about human nature, and about a changing and growing perception of The Existing One, the Name of God in human consciousness. Trust your dreams, these men tell us. Your dreams are telling you about your life.

Any summary fails to convey the depth of the writings that bear their names. Most of these prophets go around telling everyone in graphic terms how horrible things are when *ruah Elohim* is forgotten. Even though they speak for Divine Spirit, the prophets are often strange and imperfect men. The brilliant, poetic, enlightened Isaiah wanders naked in the wilderness (though not ashamed, as Adam and Eve were in Eden). He goes "into a prophetess" who conceives and bears a child.

No Escaping God

Jonah's is a story not to be missed. It's not just a story of a man living in the belly of a whale. Jonah is commentary on spiritual Creation. Jonah—to no avail—tries to escape the God of spiritual Creation who moved on the face of the waters. Illustrating further the "good" repeated in the first chapter of Genesis, the whale swallows him up for *three days* of protection until he delivers the Word of the Voice to the people of Nineveh. After finally and reluctantly fulfilling his mission, Jonah is not happy. He sits under a gourd tree and complains even about that. But Jonah appears again later in Jesus' remarks (Matthew 12:39–40), in what is perhaps one of the most important theological statements of our or any time. Those wondering about an apocalyptic end will want to take note of the verses.

Prophetic Messages

The prophets also tell the people—tell us—that the Creator of the first chapter of Genesis is the only Parent, gives conception, gives what you ask for, provides female or male companionship, is gender free, is more patient and faithful than anyone on earth, loved you before you were in your mother's womb, heals all diseases, keeps promises, feeds you in any wilderness for as long as you need, beards lions in their den, makes water, distributes equally, provides dry land—a firm place on which to stand—and is Love, Spirit, Truth, Mind, Life, Soul, All.

Isaiah calls Israel a harlot. Jeremiah, Ezekiel, Hosea, Joel, Amos, Micah, and Nahum do the same. Looking up the words *harlot* and *harlotry*, one finds these references and is not surprised that there is little or no evidence that these men were popular. They said what few or none wanted to hear. The people were unfaithful to The One Creator. If one views the prophets' association of whores with a city or nation that turns away from the One God as attacks on womanhood, one misses the point. The point is not to condemn women. Rather, the point is brought home that the Creator—and *male and female*—are inextricably linked. Further, what a nation thinks about the Creator has much to do with what a nation thinks about itself. And so the use of the word *harlot* is not just an attack on a nation's consciousness of itself but also on the idea that the Creator is the province of any particular nation.

The Bride

Isaiah, Jeremiah, and Joel speak of a bride, and, looking ahead to Revelation, the figure of woman in chapter 12 represents the struggle of all Israel—all those who strive. Biblically, we are headed in that direction and beyond, to Revelation 21:2, with its image of a pure, spiritual woman representing New Jerusalem—adorned as a bride. With that in mind, it's possible to recognize that, tiresome as these prophets may have seemed at the time, as ferocious as they often are to read, what they saw and what they say is: Beware. Don't get sidetracked. Don't leave the male and female spiritual union of Genesis 1:27 for idolatry. Lift up your eyes. Stay focused on Creation. It's where you live.

Ezekiel

Ezekiel specifically includes both women and men in his prophecies on individual responsibility and relationship to The Existing One. He also uses relationships between women and men as metaphors in prophecy. Of particular interest is chapter 16 of Ezekiel, in which the prophet uses the relationship between lovers, husband and wives, mothers and daughters and sisters to contrast the difference between Eve's descendent and the *female* of male and female in Genesis 1:27.

Chapter 17 of Ezekiel is put forth as a riddle and a parable. We see in that chapter words and images already familiar from our trip through the Bible so far: *wings, seed, vine, tree* are some. Though Ezekiel has been read as a denominational treatise on the politics and devotion of nations or as a prefiguration of Revelation, it can easily be read as an address to your own thought. Its language is the language of women's relationships, hopes, and fears.

Woman in Travail

If you are reading a Bible that contains divisions of the Hebrew Bible and the New Testament, you will see that in the last twelve books of that Bible all the images and promises and events so far in earlier chapters are recapped and prophesied. One example is when Micah says:

In that day, saith the Lord, will I assemble her that halteth, and I will gather her that is driven out, and her that I have afflicted; And I will make her that halted a remnant, and her that was cast far off a strong nation: and the Lord shall reign over them in mount Zion from henceforth, even for ever. And thou, O tower of the flock, the strong hold of the daughter of Zion, unto thee shall it come, even the first dominion; the kingdom shall come to the daughter of Jerusalem. Now why dost thou cry out aloud? is there no king in thee? is thy counsellor perished? for pangs have taken thee as a woman in travail. (Micah 4:6–9)

Two Queens

If you are afraid to stand up for yourself, Esther is a biblical role model. If you think personal happiness is the only reason to be born, she does not. Esther is the second of the two books in the Bible named for women. Like Ruth, Esther lives among foreigners. Ruth saves the day for the biological line of the children of Israel, and Esther saves the day for the people of Israel as a whole. Whereas Ruth is a Moabitess, Esther is, by birth, a Jew named Hadassah. She becomes a woman with her own holiday: her story is celebrated each year as part of Purim. The account is yet another example of how men's treatment of women can have international repercussions.

Scapegoats

Among other things, the Book of Esther describes how men in power fear women and Jews. It's got love, danger, and an upsetting of the best-laid plans of an evil, boastful, self-serving man. Esther is a great story for a rainy afternoon, and you'll do no disservice to its religious importance if you read it as a wonderful short story. There is an orphan heroine who lives in a palace. And what a palace! The descriptions of the white, green, and blue hangings, the pillars of marble, the beds of gold and silver, the floors of red, blue, white, and black marble, the gold wineglasses will take you, for a time, out of the everyday.

The device that sets up Esther's story is the demand of a husband—a king—whose heart was made merry by wine (Esther 1:10), and the refusal of his wife, Queen Vashti, to be out on public display solely for her beauty—solely as "arm candy." The reader is not told whether this female beauty is reflected in black skin or white or brown or a mixture or whether beauty is measured in height or weight. Rather, this story, and the Bible as a whole, seldom describes how women or men look but describes instead how they think, what they wonder, how they respond, and, most of all, what they do.

Ahasuerus, the king who reigned from India to Ethiopia, commanded:

> To bring Vashti the queen before the king with the crown
> royal, to shew the people and the princes her beauty: for
> she was fair to look on.
> But the queen Vashti refused to come at the king's
> commandment by his chamberlains: therefore was the king
> very wroth, and his anger burned in him. (Esther 1:11–12)

Vashti has been reexamined in recent decades. Previously characterized as disobedient, she has since been called independent and liberated. Vashti's refusal to come when she is called evokes the rage some men have when they cannot control women. The king traps himself when he makes a public call for his wife to appear at his bidding. He is humiliated in public. Rather than deal with his wife on a one-to-one basis, the king asks his wise men what to do. Although the Bible text expresses no judgment at all on Vashti's refusal, the men in power all agree that she has committed an offense, that if word gets around and other women hear of it, this will cause women to despise their husbands and "there arise too much contempt and wrath" (Esther 1:18). The men advise the king to change queens. They make a law that every man shall bear rule in his own house.

Best-Laid Plans

What are we to make of this story? Certainly these men wanted absolute control over women. They advise giving Vashti's estate to another woman. Money is a weapon, and legislation by males over women is one way they deal with their fears. But when the king's anger abates, "he remembered Vashti, and what she had done and what had been decreed against her" (Esther 2:1). The biblical use of the word *remembered* brings fulfillment. Does this mean that the king gave Vashti her own royal household? Did she take her royal belongings and move? Did she stay there? The reader is not told that Vashti lost anything but that which she did not want—an appearance before the king, who had been drinking. The fact of the text is, without Vashti's refusal there would be no room in the palace for the woman to come.

The search begins for a virgin to take the queen's place.

Enter Esther.

Her rise to power and what she did with it holds great and timeless appeal for some. Others simply can't abide Esther. The Book of Esther evokes, among other things, a strong response as to how women should act. And Vashti's refusal to come when called is mild compared to what Esther does when she has power. Had the advisors to the king known what was to come, they might have wished for Vashti.

Purpose

The most quoted and perhaps most significant line in this book of the Bible is chapter 4, verse 14:

> Who knows whether you are come to the kingdom for such a time as this?

It's a great question. In the context of the story, it relates to our connections to the rest of the human family. It can aid in reasoning on our potential and place in time. Esther is chosen out of the harem; the king loves her and makes her queen.

In the story of Esther, fear of women shifts to fear of Jews. Mordecai, a Jew and Esther's nearest living relative, refuses to bow to Haman, the king's enforcer. So Haman orders all the Jews killed. As a woman and a Jew, Esther is the potential focus of the hatred. But hatred of women or Jews is not acceptable to The Existing One who has created all good. When Mordecai lets Esther know that the order is out to kill all Jews and that includes her, he asks that challenging question: "Who knows if you did not come into the kingdom for a time such as this?"

The rest of the story is intricate and satisfying for the heroine and her people. And although, as it is widely known, the Book of Esther makes no reference to God by name, the story is replete with references that say it is taking place not only in a Middle Eastern palace-cum-harem but also in spiritual Creation. In the ten short chapters of the book are the *third day*, *the seven days*, *remembered*, *abundance*, *seed*, *light*.

Because both Vashti and Mordecai refuse to bow to secular power, some Bible readers see the story as stressing obedience to God rather than to the state. Others take the king to be a metaphor for God, or view the king and Esther as representing the masculine and feminine elements necessary for harmony and peace. Still others think Esther is a tool of men and their sexuality, but concede that, at the very least, she is in the right place at the right time. And she has a specific purpose in life—as readers do.

The Bible is about consciousness. Ask yourself: What is my purpose?

10

The Voice and Job

Hast thou entered into the springs of the sea? or hast thou walked in the search of the depth?

—Job 38:16

What if Job is not a struggle between God and the devil over a man's soul? What if the story of Job can be read as an account of how the female nature of God silences traditional theology and restores spiritual Creation to our consciousness?

Job may be traditionally thought of as the classic story in which bad things happen to good people and yet everyone lives happily ever after. The story of the man who is remembered more for his boils than for anything else is an exploration into the struggle to understand God's true nature. Not to be overlooked is the fact that in the end women are once more elevated to their natural rights.

Job is meant to represent all people who think they are doing just fine, judging life by outward appearances. But the loss of outward goods, reputation, and family forces Job to confront the God beyond outward appearances of "right and wrong." The trigger for Job's struggle is the notion that there is an adversary who "goes to and fro upon the earth" (Job 1:7).

Whereas once the tale of Job was used to justify a vexing God who tests men and women or visits bad things on good people, Job's experience is now most often viewed as taking place in his own thoughts. And scholars now view Job's "three friends," who commiserate and blame him for his fate, as aspects of Job's own thinking—that he is entertaining conflicting views.

Job's Fear

> For Job thought, "Perhaps my children have sinned and blas-
> phemed God in their thoughts." This is what Job always used
> to do. (Job 1:5 TNK)

Job is afraid for his children, and when he receives reports—
and they are only reports—that he has lost everything, he tears his
clothes, shaves his head, and falls on the ground and worships. Job
has lost his seven sons and three daughters, his money, his health,
and—equally as fearsome to him and more to his friends—his good
name in the community. As Job puts it: "For the thing which I
greatly feared has come upon me" (Job 3:25).

Once the situation is set up, it takes over thirty chapters for Job
to lament, question, and examine what he believes has happened to
him and what, if anything, he can do about it. This is meant to be
a public discourse. Job wants everyone to know his agony. "Oh that
my words were now written! oh that they were printed in a book"
(Job: 19:23).

The Bible continually illustrates that transformations in the life
of people require a transformation in how to understand and name
God. As it was for Avram before The Breasted One renamed him
Abraham, as it was for Jacob/Israel, so will it be for Job. Job will be
transformed by his encounter with the God of all Creation. When
Job encounters the Almighty—The Breasted One, the female nature of God known to the patriarchs—he comes to himself. He no
longer struggles with self-pity, fear, theology, and the male social
order. The story of the man, Job, is actually an exploration into the
struggle to understand and acknowledge the female nature of the
Creator and all its infinite power.

Robert Sacks, in his book *The Book of Job with Commentary: A
Translation for Our Time* (2000), says that in a certain sense all the
changes in Job and his education and in the thoughts of the four

friends are reflected in musings on the womb and belly and, beginning in chapter 38, the bursting forth of spiritual Creation.

The first set of musings begins (here in Sacks's translations):
"Naked came I out of my mother's belly and naked I shall return
there" (Job 1:21). Further, there is "Why did I not come out of the
womb and die, exit the belly and perish?" (Job 3:9) and, "The womb
will forget him and the worms will find him sweet" (Job 24:20).
When Job wonders what he should do when God does come to
speak to him about the treatment of his servants: "What shall I
answer? . . . did not one fashion us in the womb?" (Job 31:14–15).
The preoccupation with the womb is an almost endless theme for
Job, notes Sacks.

Before the entry of the Voice of God into the text, the musings view the womb as empty, in some cases as a source of hatred,
rage, and contention, in others the beginning of all that is comforting. In the past, the central argument of the book was perceived to be a theological wrestling with the question: "Shall a
man be more just than his God?" (Job 4:17). Now we know that
the central fact of the book's story is about *ruah Elohim* and the
continuing revelation of Herself and Her Creation, spelled out in
chapter 38 of Job.

But first there is announcement by a fourth friend—Elihu—
who has entered the text late in the game. He gives an introduction to a loving, kind, Creative God: "Behold, God is mighty, and
despiseth not any; he is mighty in strength and wisdom" (Job
36:5). Later, Elihu ends his presentation of God: "Thus mortals
hold in FEAR the one whom even the wise in heart have never
seen" (Job 37:24). This is the last time in the text that the word
mortal appears and the last voice in the text to use the word *fear*.
The notion of mortals subject to the whims of chance and fate
is silenced. The Voice in the Tempest will never use the word
mortal.

Out of the darkness of Job's theological wrestling comes this
challenging, provocative Voice:

And the Lord answered Job out of the Tempest and said: Who is this that darkens my counsel with words without knowledge? Brace yourself like a man; I will question you, and you shall answer me. (Job 38:2–3 NIV)

It is no longer Job who will question God. It is God who will question Job. This Voice from the Tempest, the whirlwind, is a feminine noun, a feminine call, reminding Job of his own first musings: "May the day of my birth be lost and with it that night in which it was said a hero has been conceived" (Job 3:1 Sacks Translation).

The Voice sends out a barrage of questions to Job, here in the King James Version:

Where wast thou when I laid the foundations of the earth? declare, if thou hast understanding.

Who hath laid the measures thereof, if thou knowest? or who hath stretched the line upon it?

Whereupon are the foundations thereof fastened? or who laid the corner stone thereof; When the morning stars sang together, and all the sons of God shouted for joy?

Or who shut up the sea with doors, when it brake forth, as if it had issued out of the womb?

When I made the cloud the garment thereof, and thick darkness a swaddlingband for it? (Job 38:4–9)

This is primordial Creation, God as midwife making the "cloud the garment" and thick darkness a "swaddlingband." This is a nurturing God inviting Job, and us, to drop in for a visit and see the wonders and the glory of the days of that outline of Creation in the first chapter of Genesis and to become the hero, the spiritual male and female, we are originally conceived to be. We catch a glimpse of the male and female Origin as equal when the Voice says: "By what way is the light parted? Hath the rain a father? Or who hath begotten the drops of dew? Out of whose womb came the ice? And the hoary frost of heaven, who hath gendered it?" (Job 38:24, 28–29).

In fact, the Voice is reprising Its Creation in these last chapters of the Book of Job, and the challenging questions refer backward and forward to the days of Creation illumined in the first chapter of Genesis. There is the darkness out of which Job is drawn and the water of the first day in "Hast thou entered into the treasures of the snow? or hast thou seen the treasures of the hail, which I have reserved against the time of trouble, against the day of battle and war?" (Job 38:22, 23). There is reference to the stars of the fourth day of Creation: "Canst thou bind the sweet influences of Pleiades, or loose the bands of Orion? Canst thou bring forth Mazzaroth in his season? Or canst thou guide Arcturus with his sons?" (Job 38:31–32). The Pleiades are also known as the Seven Sisters in the heavens, and the constellations and lights of the fourth day of Creation are equally gendered by the Voice speaking to Job.

Each day of the first chapter of Genesis is reprised by the Voice in Job chapters 38–39, and this is all traceable with just a small amount of comparison of Genesis 1 to Job 38 and beyond. The bottom line for the questions from the Voice is, in effect, "everything was Created by Me and you are the culmination of that Creation."

"Deck now thyself with majesty and excellency; and array thyself with glory and beauty" (Job 40:10).

It is the whirling, birthing tempest or whirlwind that speaks to Job. It is a nurturing God holding in each being the identity of Itself. Job, who had once lived in a narrow world of men's mores, codes, and limited views of Deity, who had "spoken without understanding," has seen the bursting forth of Creation and now speaks back to the Voice, saying, "I know that you can do every thing and that no thought can be withheld from thee" (Job 42:1).

All's Well That Ends Well

"Thus the Lord blessed the latter years of Job's life more than the former. He had fourteen thousand sheep, six thousand camels, one thousand yoke of oxen, and one thousand she asses. He also had seven sons and three daughters. The first he named Jemimah."

Jemimah means "dove"—a reference also found in Noah sending the dove out of the Ark and in the word used for the Holy Spirit. The second daughter is named Keziah, cassia, the name of a fragrant bark of a tree. The third is named Keren-happuch—the Horn of Mascara, but it means so much more than horn; it also means "to shine," "a ray of light," "a central role in the place of worship," and—a reference to Hannah's song—"The Horn of my Salvation." "Nowhere in the land were women as beautiful as Job's daughters to be found. . . . Their father gave them estates together with their brothers" (Job 42:14, 15 TNK). Beauty here also means *good*, and nothing is said about husbands or dowries.

The new Job—the one who has seen the treasures of the snow, the way the light parts, the stars in order, the animals and plants as they truly are, and heard the female voice of Creation—has established the right of women to own and hold property. This is part of the legacy Job has brought back from the infinite world of Creation—and apposite to the male theology of his narrow and earlier days before wrestling with and confronting the Voice.

Job's fear is gone. His children are alive, and his daughters and sons both receive inheritance. In the consciousness of the Creator, of Spirit, male and female are equal, and in Job's account—as in the first chapter of Genesis—"female" is the final idea mentioned.

Afterward, Job lived one hundred and forty years to see four generations.

So Job died old and contented, satisfied with Creation.

11

Crying in the Wilderness

I will say to the north, Give up; and to the south, Keep not
back: bring my sons from far, and my daughters from the ends of
the earth . . .

—Isaiah 43:6

Who is your husband? Isaiah answers that question and more.
The Book of Isaiah speaks to all people in all times: "Learn to do
well; seek judgment, relieve the oppressed, judge the fatherless,
plead for the widow" (Isaiah 1:17).

The sixty-six chapters of the Book of Isaiah include references
to the entire Bible—references to everything from spiritual Creation to Adam and Eve and to the Book of Revelation. There are
references to Abraham and Sarah, Egypt, the Commandments, the
cloud, the *tabernacle*, Israel, the *woman in travail*, cities, the practice
of religion, and the fulfillment of prophecy. There are references to
the "new heaven and the new earth," and to "wiping away all tears
from the eyes." There are parables, visions, oracles, and promises.
Isaiah is a book for everyone.

Early on, in chapter 2 verse 22, Isaiah starts urging people to
give up their belief in Adam. "Cease ye from man whose breath is
in his nostrils. For wherein is he to be accounted of," says the King
James Version. The Tanakh has this as "Oh cease to glorify man,
who has only a breath in his nostrils! For by what does he merit
esteem?"

So much for Adam, created not by *ruah Elohim*, but who was
made "alive" in Genesis 2:7: "And the Lord God formed man of the
dust of the ground, and breathed into his nostrils the breath of life."

Mother

Moving on, or back, from Adam, Isaiah does give comfort. Although early on Isaiah challenges Adam as the man of God's creating, toward the end of his writings The Existing One—through Isaiah—assures us: "As one whom his mother comforteth, so will I comfort you; and ye shall be comforted in Jerusalem" (Isaiah 66:13).

On the way to that statement there is this: "Since thou was precious in my sight, thou hast been honorable, and I have loved thee: therefore will I give men for thee, and people for thy life. Fear not: for I am with thee: I will bring thy seed from the east, and gather thee from the west; I will say to the north, Give up; and to the south, Keep not back: bring my sons from afar, and my daughters from the ends of the earth" (Isaiah 43:4–6).

Inspired by Isaiah are words from Handel's *Messiah*.

Comfort ye, comfort ye my people, saith your God.
(Isaiah 40:1)
    O Zion, that bringeth good tidings, get thee up into
the high mountain; O Jerusalem, that bringest good tidings,
lift up thy voice with strength; lift it up, be not afraid: say
into the cities of Judah, Behold your God! (Isaiah 40:9)

Jerusalem is not only a geographic location but defined by the Strong's definition as "teaching of peace."

Husband

Chapter 54 of Isaiah says:

Enlarge the place of thy tent, and let them stretch forth the
curtains of thine habitations: spare not, lengthen thy cords,
and strengthen thy stakes;
    Fear not; for thou shalt not be ashamed: neither be thou
confounded; for thou shalt not be put to shame: for thou shalt

forget the shame of thy youth, and shalt not remember the reproach of thy widowhood any more.

For thy Maker is thine husband:

For the Lord hath called thee as a woman forsaken and grieved in spirit, and a wife of youth, when thou wast refused, saith thy God. (54:2–6)

Woman in Travail

The last chapter of Isaiah, chapter 66, repeats the theme of the woman in travail:

Who hath heard such a thing? who hath seen such things? Shall the earth be made to bring forth in one day? or shall a nation be born at once? for as soon as Zion travailed, she brought forth her children.

Shall I bring to the birth, and not cause to bring forth? saith the Lord: shall I cause to bring forth, and shut the womb? saith thy God.

Rejoice ye with Jerusalem, and be glad with her, all ye that love her: rejoice for joy with her, all ye that mourn for her:

That ye may suck, and be satisfied with the breasts of her consolations, that ye may milk out, and be delighted with the abundance of her glory. (Isaiah 66:8–11)

Isaiah is prophetic and speaks of a Mothering God available to all.

Deep Waters

There are those days when moods can overtake you. There are those days in life when nothing works, when unrequited love, sadness, depression, and despair seem to be the entire landscape of thought. What you want is not there and what you usually do to get yourself out of it—a hot bath, a long talk with a friend, television, the Internet or a movie, shopping, work, a run, a meaningless social encounter—isn't available or doesn't work.

Perhaps you feel as if Adam and Eve really did bring punishment through the ages—right down to your doorstep. You seem stuck in strange genetic coding traits inherited from your family through the generations, convinced almost that genes are programmed to use human beings to secure the continuity of genes themselves. And this leaves you helpless and hopeless.

Love and Sex

Curl up in bed with the Song of Songs. (If your Bible doesn't have this book, go find a Bible that does.) The eight chapters that make up this book are full of joy, intimacy, physical description of passion, and sensuousness. Whether one reads it "straight" as it is written or takes it to be an allegory of God's love for Israel, the Song of Songs or the Song of Solomon (that great lover), as the King James Version has it, is sexually explicit. And the body is celebrated.

All in all this is a book for the imaginative woman. It resounds with love. Curling up in bed with the Song of Songs, lingering over the detailed descriptions one finds there, provides eroticism with inspiration. The text is as juicy as that of a popular novel and much more descriptive in imagery. There is no shame in the Song of Songs. No sin. No guilt. No Eve. Kisses, delights, sweet smells, anticipation, eagerness—the text spills over with desire for the love and the beloved.

This centerpiece of the Hebrew Bible is required reading for anyone who thinks the Book is a proscriptive sexist text. Imagine, if you choose, God as your lover, or you and your lover as worshipping God together, or read it any way you want. Excerpts don't do it justice. Read it for yourself. No one is looking over your shoulder. The text speaks directly to you.

A Completely Other Approach

If the Song of Songs isn't an antidote to whatever ails you, throw yourself into the Book of Lamentations. It speaks directly to women who are burdened. It recognizes the way you feel, and that recognition takes away the sting of being misunderstood and abandoned. Just the first six verses of Lamentations address the state of widowhood, weeping, loss of lovers, friends who betray, life among the heathen, children in captivity to enemies, faded beauty, and lack of leadership.

> How doth the city sit solitary, that was full of people! How is she become as a widow! she that was great among the nations, and princess among the provinces, how is she become tributary! She weepeth sore in the night, and her tears are on her cheeks: among all her lovers she hath none to comfort her: all her friends have dealt treacherously with her, they are become her enemies.
>
> Judah is gone into captivity because of affliction, and because of great servitude: she dwelleth among the heathen, she findeth no rest: all her persecutors overtook her between the straits. The ways of Zion do mourn, because none come to the solemn feasts: all her gates are desolate: her priests sigh, her virgins are afflicted, and she is in bitterness. Her adversaries are the chief, her enemies prosper; for the Lord hath afflicted her for the multitude of her transgressions: her children are gone into captivity before the enemy. And from the daughter of Zion all her beauty is departed: her princes are become like harts that find no pasture, and they are gone without strength before the pursuer. (Lamentations 1:1–6)

Loss

Read yearly in temple during midsummer on the ninth of Av (Tishah B'Av), Lamentations commemorates, in a mournful celebration, the destruction of the First and Second Temples. But a more immediate significance to Lamentations can be found when one looks at the themes of destruction and loss in a very personal sense. Read as it is written with all the instances of "she" and "her," and the female imagery seems to empathize with the reader.

Lamentations says that there are things in life to weep over and that when those days come,

> Their heart cried unto the Lord, O wall of the daughter of Zion, let tears run down like a river day and night: give thyself no rest; let not the apple of thine eye cease. (Lamentations 2:18)

If you have ever felt this way:

> For these things I weep; mine eye, mine eye runneth down with water, because the comforter that should relieve my soul is far from me: my children are desolate, because the enemy prevailed. (Lamentations 1:16)

then Lamentations can be an empathetic companion.

Always Hope

But after a little wallowing, things look up by chapter 3.

> This I recall to my mind, therefore have I hope.
> It is of the Lord's mercies that we are not consumed, because his compassions fail not. They are new every morning: great is thy faithfulness. (Lamentations 3:21–23)

The ebbing and flowing of moods, thoughts, and experience is plain in Lamentations. Things were once great, then they are terrible, then they get better, then worse again. By the end of the book there is a balance of thought, an acceptance. In your darkest hours, read Lamentations and see if the same thing doesn't happen for you. Read not as history, not as condemnation of women, rather as a voice through the ages that understands your mourning, your need, Lamentations can at least, in its sense of suffering and loss, bring you face to face with the honest recognition that if things can't get any worse, then they have to get better.

As a Woman in Travail

Lamentations is properly called the Lamentations of Jeremiah. Jeremiah lived during the reign of King Josiah, and it is more than interesting to note that at that time, Huldah, a female, interpreted the Law (Torah), and Jeremiah, a male, prophesied in female imagery.

Jeremiah is often depicted as a frightening figure. But his first report of the word of The Existing One is that of Primal Mother: "Before I formed thee in the belly I knew thee; and before thou camest forth out of the womb I sanctified thee, and I ordained thee a prophet unto the nations" (Jeremiah 1:5).

Jeremiah makes seven references to the woman in travail (all the following are from the King James Version):

> For I have heard a voice as of a woman in travail, and the anguish as of her that bringeth forth her first child, the voice of the daughter of Zion, that bewaileth herself, that spreadeth her hands, saying, Woe is me now! for my soul is wearied because of murderers. (4:31)
>
> We have heard the fame thereof: our hands wax feeble: anguish hath taken hold of us, and pain, as of a woman in travail. (6:24)
>
> What wilt thou say when he shall punish thee? for thou hast taught them to be captains, and as chief over thee: shall not sorrows take thee, as a woman in travail? (13:21)
>
> O inhabitant of Lebanon, that makest thy nest in the cedars, how gracious shalt thou be when pangs come upon thee, the pain as of a woman in travail! (22:23)

Damascus is waxed feeble, and turneth herself to flee, and fear hath seized on her: anguish and sorrows have taken her, as a woman in travail. (49:24)

The king of Babylon hath heard the report of them, and his hands waxed feeble: anguish took hold of him, and pangs as of a woman in travail. (50:43)

And more of the loving aspect of The Existing One comes from Jeremiah. "The Lord hath appeared of old unto me, saying, Yea, I have loved thee with an everlasting love: therefore with loving-kindness have I drawn thee" (Jeremiah 31:3).

In the Heart of the Temple

What if the Bible says a priest and king have to go to a woman to find out what the Word of God actually says?

This is the story of Huldah.

Huldah is a prophetess, the chosen voice of God. Her story is told twice in almost identical words in two different books of the Bible—2 Kings and 2 Chronicles. King Josiah has been shown the Book of the Law, which has been lost and then found during repairs to the House of God. Josiah, still in his twenties when he is shown the rediscovered Law, rends his clothes when he hears its words. Looking for the true interpretation of the teaching, he sends men who represent different classes of society—a priest, a scribe, a servant, and two other men—saying, "Go and inquire of the Lord for me, and for the people and for all Judah, concerning the words of this book that is found" (2 Kings 22:13).

To Huldah is where they go to find the voice of The True Existing One, not only for the king but also for the priests, the servants, and the scribes, and for all Judah. Huldah is dwelling in "Jerusalem in the college" (2 Kings 22:14). She speaks for Spirit, God, and, according to the biblical text, she looks to be the only person on earth who can interpret the Word.

And she said unto them, Thus saith the Lord God of Israel,
Tell the man that sent you to me,

Thus saith the Lord, Behold, I will bring evil upon this
place, and upon the inhabitants thereof, even all the words
of the book which the king of Judah hath read: Because they
have forsaken me, and have burned incense unto other gods,
that they might provoke me to anger with all the works of
their hands; therefore my wrath shall be kindled against this
place, and shall not be quenched.

But to the king of Judah which sent you to inquire of the
Lord, thus shall ye say to him, Thus saith the Lord God of
Israel, As touching the words which thou hast heard; Because
thine heart was tender, and thou hast humbled thyself before
the Lord, when thou heardest what I spake against this place,
and against the inhabitants thereof, that they should become
a desolation and a curse, and hast rent thy clothes, and wept
before me; I also have heard thee, saith the Lord.

Behold therefore, I will gather thee unto thy fathers, and
thou shalt be gathered into thy grave in peace; and thine eyes
shall not see all the evil which I will bring upon this place.
And they brought the king word again. (2 Kings 22:15–20)

According to Marvin Sweeney in his book *King Josiah of Judah*
(2001):

Josiah is a figure of extraordinary importance for the history of
ancient Israel and Judah. According to the biblical narrative,
a Torah scroll was discovered during the renovation of the
Jerusalem Temple in the eighteenth year of Josiah's reign.
This scroll, commonly identified as a form of Deuteronomy,
became the basis of an ambitious program of religious reform
and national restoration in which Josiah closed down all
pagan worship sites throughout the land of Israel, centralized
worship at the Jerusalem Temple, and attempted to reunite

Israel and Judah as an independent monarchy under the rule of the royal house of David. (2001; online at http://www .oxfordscholarship.com/oso/public/content/religion/ 0195133242/toc.html)

Huldah Changes a Kingdom

Huldah's hearing and speaking for Divinity causes a turnaround in the thinking, observances, and practices of the entire kingdom— and causes the king to put magicians, wizards, and idols out of the land. "There was no king before or after him, The Bible says, that turned to the Lord with all his heart, and with all his soul, and with all his might, according to the law of Moses" (2 Kings 23:23–25). Thanks to Huldah.

The Bible itself sets aside the idea that women can't (or have not until our times) interpret the Bible. The Bible makes clear in this account that a woman is fully qualified to understand, interpret, and speak for The Supreme Creator and Ruler. For those readers who might enjoy digging into this profoundly important record of a woman who interprets the holy texts of Israel, there is more about the Huldah story, a repeated form, in 2 Chronicles 34.

Different Offices

Along with Sarah, Miriam, Deborah, Hannah, Abigail, and Esther, Huldah is one of the seven woman prophets of Israel. Each of the women reflects a different saving aspect of *ruah Elohim.* Huldah's prophetic place in Scripture, however, differs from that of the other women prophets in that Huldah is the only one who unveils God's meaning directly from the text. The Hebrew Bible closes two chapters after the story of Huldah and the implications of her interpretation. Note that whereas the Hebrew Bible closes with 2 Chronicles, the Old Testament of the King James Version closes with Malachi.

But if one reads the Bible as a whole, with its implications for international policy and the health of women, there is more to come. We turn now to the Gospels and the New Testament, which recount the life and works of Jesus of Nazareth—Jesus Christ— describes the history of the early church, and depicts in the Book of Revelation, the *pure river of life, the woman in travail*, the struggle for consciousness and *the teaching of peace*—Jerusalem.

12

The Eyewitnesses

But Mary kept all these things, and pondered them in her heart.
—Luke 2:19

The fundamental question of the four Gospels and the New Testament is: What do you think about Jesus? It's the question he asks his disciples in Mark's Gospel—"and by the way he asked his disciples, saying unto them, Whom do men say that I am?" (Mark 8:27). And in Luke 22:70: "Then said they all, Art thou then the Son of God? And he said unto them, Ye say that I am."

Whatever one thinks about the person Jesus, the Gospels and the New Testament present his story—often told to the scribes by women. Jesus' life is there in one form or another from the beginning genealogy of Matthew to the end, at the Book of Revelation. But it is in the Book of John that Jesus answers the questions about himself:

My Father worketh hitherto, and I work. (5:17)

I am the living bread which came down from heaven. (6:51)

Before Abraham was, I Am. (8:58)

I am the light of the world. (9:5)

I am the good shepherd. (10:11)

I and my Father are one. (10:30)

I am the way, the truth, and the life. (14:6)

I am the true vine, and my Father is the husbandman.
(15:1)

The life of Jesus the Christ or Christ Jesus (Jesus, as in Joshua, meaning "Savior"; Christ meaning "anointed one," or Messiah) is told in many ways. Four different versions of Jesus' life, work, and sayings address four different ways of thinking; these four versions are called the *Gospels*—a word that means "good news." The authors tell us some (but not all) of the same stories about Jesus, but they are told from quite different perspectives.

The last Gospel—the Gospel of John—begins with the spiritual Creation of the first chapter of Genesis. "In the beginning was the Word and the Word was with God, and the word was God" is the King James Version of John 1:1. The word *beginning* is a feminine noun transliterated from the Greek to Arche. Not only is the Word defined as speaking, naming, calling out, but in Greek, *logos*, this Word echoes Genesis in "and God said" and "God called" *light, day, heavens.* John talks about Light; then he introduces John the Baptist, and by chapter 2 (with no discussion of Jesus' birth or youth) has us at the opening of Jesus' ministry, in which, at the behest of his mother, he turns water into wine.

Sources

The first Gospel is the Gospel of Matthew. His account of Jesus begins with a genealogical list of the generations of Jesus Christ—Abraham to Jesus, forty-two in all. And then there is a brief account of the birth of Jesus from the point of view of Joseph. By placing Jesus in a biological line of "begats," Matthew's version reflects a biological mindset.

Matthew is the only one of the four Gospel authors who recounts a trip to Egypt to save the baby Jesus from Herod. Matthew 2:13–16 is a reprise of Joseph of Genesis, who rescued his brothers and fathers and all the tribes of Israel by bringing them to Egypt. It is Matthew who repeats Jeremiah's statement: "Rachel weeping for her children" (Matthew 2:18).

In the Gospel of Mark, he says that he talked to Jesus' disciple Peter. Mark's version begins with John the Baptist clothed with camel hair and a girdle of skin about his loins, eating locusts and wild honey and "preaching in the wilderness the baptism of repentance" as he announces the appearance of one "who shall baptize you with the Holy Ghost" (Mark 1:2–8). In Mark's account, Jesus makes his entrance as a full-grown man. Mark gives no record of any part of Jesus' childhood or adolescence.

Luke's account is not as metaphysical as John's, not as worldly as Matthew's, and not as concise as Mark's. Luke says he interviewed the eyewitnesses (Luke 1:2), and he addresses his Gospel to "friend of God"—Theophilus in Greek. Translators have spent time trying to identify who this man, Theophilus, was; they seem not to have considered the meaning of the word as indicative of an address to any who count themselves, like Abraham, a "friend of God." (Luke also addresses the Book of Acts to come to "friends of God.") Many of the eyewitnesses were women, and Luke's account reflects that, offering information known only to the women or a particular woman. Luke's account begins with Elisabeth and her conception of John the Baptist. Elisabeth is a descendent of Miriam and Moses' brother, Aaron, and she is cousin to Mary, soon to be the mother of Jesus. Mary's response to the angelic announcement that she will conceive appears in Luke.

Did the Angel Appear to Joseph or to Mary?

Matthew says that an unnamed angel appeared to Joseph in a dream. Luke says the angel Gabriel visited Mary at her home. Luke begins with the story of Elisabeth and her husband Zacharias— meaning "remembered by God" (Luke 1:5–25).

Elisabeth is barren and, as was Sarah, of advanced age. An angel appears to her husband, Zacharias, and tells him that she will bear a son who must be named John. And this is not to be just any son, but one "who is great in the sight of the Lord"—so translates the King James Version. But the original word translated as "Lord" is *Kurios*, which means God, or one who has the power of deciding.

Zacharias questions the angel and wants to know how he will know this message is true. The angel answers,

> I am Gabriel, that stand in the presence of God; and am sent to speak unto thee, and to shew thee these glad tidings. And, behold, thou shalt be dumb, and not able to speak, until the day that these things shall be performed, because thou believest not my words, which shall be fulfilled in their season. And the people waited for Zacharias, and marvelled that he tarried so long in the temple. And when he came out, he could not speak unto them: and they perceived that he had seen a vision in the temple: for he beckoned unto them, and remained speechless. (Luke 1:19–22)

Elisabeth keeps herself shut up for five months—perhaps to avoid neighbors' gossip and speculation, perhaps to ponder and protect this great event in her life. In the sixth month of her pregnancy, the angel Gabriel comes from God to Mary and says, "'Hail, thou that art highly favoured, the Lord is with thee: blessed art thou among women.' And when she saw him, she was troubled at his saying, and cast in her mind what manner of salutation this should be" (Luke 1:28–29). Phillips translates Luke 1:29 as "Mary was deeply perturbed at these words and wondered what such a greeting could possibly mean."

And the angel says to her what Elijah said to the widow, what the angel said to Hagar, what Gabriel said to Zacharias, what angels say throughout time: "Fear not." Then comes the announcement that she will have a child, who will reign over the house of Jacob forever. Mary asks the question still asked today: "How shall this be, seeing I know not a man?" Gabriel explains: "The Holy Ghost shall come upon thee, and the power of the Highest shall overshadow thee" (Luke 1:34–35).

Creation

For "proof in the flesh," Gabriel tells her about Elisabeth and adds the line that says it all: "For with God nothing shall be impossible."

Echoing Ruth and Hannah and Abigail, Mary says, "Behold the handmaid of the Lord, be it unto me according to thy word" (Luke 1:38). Phillips has an interesting translation: "I belong to the Lord, body and soul, let it happen as you say."

What Mary does next makes such sense that it is hard to believe that Luke did not get this story from Mary herself. She gets up and goes to see Elisabeth, her cousin. Put in the context of what life is actually like, what must it have been to be these women, speculating together for three months on their pregnancies, their children, their future, the price of these two conceptions? See where Elisabeth says to Mary, "blessed is the fruit of thy womb." Does it refer to Creation? "And God said, Let the earth bring forth grass, the herb yielding seed, and the fruit tree yielding fruit after his kind, whose seed is in itself, upon the earth: and it was so" (Genesis 1:11–13).

The Bible says later by way of further explication: "But God giveth it a body as it has pleased him, to every seed his own body" (1 Corinthians 15:38).

Mary paraphrases Hannah's song in her response to Elisabeth:

My soul doth magnify the Lord,
    And my spirit hath rejoiced in God my Saviour.
    For he hath regarded the low estate of his handmaiden:
for, behold, from henceforth all generations shall call me
blessed.
    For he that is mighty hath done to me great things;
and holy is his name.
    And his mercy is on them that fear him from generation
to generation.
    He hath shewed strength with his arm; he hath scattered
the proud in the imagination of their hearts.
    He hath put down the mighty from their seats, and
exalted them of low degree.
    He hath filled the hungry with good things; and the rich
he hath sent empty away. He hath holpen his servant Israel,
in remembrance of his mercy;

As he spake to our fathers, to Abraham, and to his seed for ever. (Luke 1:46–55)

After abiding together three months, the women part.

Mother Chooses Name

Mary returns to her house and the story turns to the birth and naming of Elisabeth's child:

When the eighth day came, they were going to circumcise the child and call him Zacharias, after his father, but his mother said, "Oh no! he must be called John." But none of your relations is called John, they replied. (Luke 1:59–61 Phillips)

Although the bystanders in the temple where the scene takes place may not understand, the reader knows that the child is not the product solely of biological reproduction. His name—"to whom Jehovah is gracious"—is meant to reflect that spiritual conception. Still they asked his father what he wanted for a name. He wrote on a writing-tablet—"His name is John"—and then the power of his speech came back.

Not long after that, Mary brought forth her firstborn son. Almost all know the account of the manger: "no room at the inn . . . shepherds abiding in the field . . . the angel of the Lord . . . the glory of the Lord shone round about them . . . good tidings of great joy . . . a multitude of the heavenly host praising God and saying . . . on earth peace, good will to men." All this is described only by Luke (2:8–14).

"But Mary kept all these things, and pondered them in her heart" (Luke 2:19).

Women and Jesus

Because the central figure of Christianity is male, do women have to bow down to all men? Because the central figure is male, are women left without viable roles models for a spiritual path?

Searching the accounts of Jesus' life, one finds no restrictions on gender— either in the person of Jesus himself or in his dealings with women. Those women who might express themselves by saying that they feel confined by Jesus' maleness must first ask if they are troubled by the Bible's accounts of Jesus or the accounts of the historical church. Searching the accounts of Jesus' life, we find nothing there that says women cannot be priests or disciples or ministers. Still, no reader with an open mind will be satisfied with the patronizing attitude that says: Jesus treated women well, so what's the problem?

Why, some wonder, can't all men be like him—treating women as full and equal expressions of the spiritual Creator? The answer may not be to romanticize Jesus and, by contrast, find the men in one's life a major disappointment. To consider the enormity of the issue involved and to look toward where the answer lives, we may bring in Paul, who says in Colossians: "When Christ, who is our life, shall appear, then shall ye also appear with him in glory" (Colossians 3:4). Paul does not say, "When Jesus appears again" but rather references the Christ—the Divine Nature. It's still rather a mystery, as Paul will say later in a letter to Ephesians in which he muses on Adam and Eve.

There are few who are not at least familiar with Jesus' encounters with women, and scriptural references abound.

The baby Jesus is to be circumcised. Luke's report puts us in the temple with Simeon, waiting for "the consolation of Israel: and the Holy Ghost was upon him" (Luke 2:25). And, as Luke rarely tells a story about a man without then telling about a woman, we see Anna, a prophetess. She is of the tribe of Asher, and she is a widow of great age (about eighty-four); Luke says, "she has served God with prayer and fastings night and day and, coming into the temple at that instant, she gave thanks to the Lord and spoke to all of them for the redemption of Jerusalem"—the teaching of peace (Luke 2:36–38).

Luke records Jesus' visit to the temple at the age of twelve. "And all that heard him were astonished at his understanding and answers" (Luke 2:47). Upon Mary's discovery of him there, Jesus declares to his mother: "wist ye not that I must be about my Father's business?" (Luke 2:49). It is not until after Jesus is baptized by John the Baptist, not until after "the Holy Ghost descended in a bodily shape like a dove and a voice came from heaven, which said, Thou art my beloved Son" that Luke says: "And Jesus himself began to be about thirty years of age. Being (as was supposed) the son of Joseph" (Luke 3:23).

After three chapters of conception, angels, births, Luke begins a biological genealogy of Jesus. Both Matthew and Luke—the two of the four Gospel writers who include genealogies—list women in their recounting of "begats." But in Luke, the genealogies come after the accounts of the divinely formed conceptions of Mary and her cousin.

Women Ministering

Luke says that the political, economic, and social temptations that Jesus faces in the wilderness (Luke 4:1–16) preface his return to Galilee in the power of the Spirit—the same Spirit that moved upon the face of the waters in the first chapter of Genesis. Reading aloud in his hometown synagogue, Jesus' reference to himself as previously announced in the book of Isaiah stuns the people. But nothing makes people so angry as to hear this:

> But I tell you of a truth, many widows were in Israel in the days of Elias, when the heaven was shut up three years and six months, when great famine was throughout all the land;
>
> But unto none of them was Elias sent, save unto Sarepta, a city of Sidon, unto a woman that was a widow. And many lepers were in Israel in the time of Eliseus the prophet; and none of them was cleansed, saving Naaman the Syrian.

When they heard these things, they were filled with wrath,

And rose up, and thrust him out of the city, and led him unto the brow of the hill whereon their city was built, that they might cast him down headlong.

But he passing through the midst of them went his way. (Luke 4:24–30)

Highlighting women and the afflicted, as Jesus does in reading Isaiah, angers many now as then. Luke's Gospel continues the themes of Isaiah and Jesus in a focus on women and the afflicted. Luke's Gospel is a case study in gender balance, and egalitarianism. Not only does Luke say the angel appeared to Mary and not to Joseph, but he is the only Gospel author to give background on Jesus' youth.

Equal Treatment

Luke's stories about men and women alternate. For example, when Jesus leaves the synagogue and passes through the midst of a crowd, he first rebukes and casts devils out of a man and then heals the mother-in-law of Simon (Peter) by "rebuking a great fever" (Luke 4:38). He then heals any and all of the sick brought to him (Luke 4:40). The pattern here is man, then woman, then all, echoing the sixth day of Creation in the first chapter of Genesis.

After a feast given for Jesus in a "great house," Luke records that Jesus talked of the "children of the bridechamber and the bridegroom," spoke of sewing while alluding to spiritual Creation, and talked about wine—new and old (Luke 5:29–39). In the first half of chapter 7, he heals a man who is not physically present, and then, as Elijah did, restores to a widow that which was lost by raising her son from the dead. And then again, "he cured many of their infirmities" (Luke 7:21). Jesus answers men's questions about how to tell whether or not he is the One Who Is to Come by his healing works. They say,

John Baptist hath sent us unto thee, saying, Art thou he that should come? or look we for another? And in that same hour he cured many of their infirmities and plagues, and of evil spirits; and unto many that were blind he gave sight.

Then Jesus answering said unto them, Go your way, and tell John what things ye have seen and heard; how that the blind see, the lame walk, the lepers are cleansed, the deaf hear, the dead are raised, to the poor the gospel is preached. (Luke 7:20–22)

Seeing Women

Surely the best-known story of women and Jesus is the story Luke tells in chapter 7:36–50 of the woman who—at an otherwise all-male dinner—washes Jesus' feet. Though she is unnamed, she has been called Mary Magdala, and she has had a long history at the hands of commentators, actresses, and novelists from the time that Luke wrote his Gospel to today. That she has no name underlies the timelessness of the story. The woman is unnamed not because she is unimportant but because, by virtue of being unnamed, she could be any of us.

To insist that she is Mary Magdalene hides the essence of the story by localizing sin and forgiveness in a sexual context.

In the style Luke uses to report—alternating the stories of the genders and then including both male and female together—the story is a model of humility and an exposé of sexism. It is the woman, not the host, who washes the guest Jesus' feet. Water, that central biblical theme, is found in her tears. Fulfilling the function of priest, she anoints Jesus' feet and washes them with her tears.

The Pharisee who is the host of this dinner says to himself that if Jesus were a prophet, he would know that the woman washing his feet was a "sinner."

To read the story as simply detailing the customs of religions whereby men, monks, and prophets are not to be touched by women is to miss the point. The story is about how men view women through the lens of sexuality. It is at that point that Jesus, reading the host's unspoken thought, says, "Seest thou this woman?" (Luke 7:44). He begins to reiterate what the woman has done since she entered the room—and what the host has not done.

> I entered into thine house, thou gavest me no water for
> my feet: but she hath washed my feet with tears, and wiped
> them with the hairs of her head.
>   Thou gavest me no kiss: but this woman since the time
> I came in hath not ceased to kiss my feet. My head with oil
> thou didst not anoint: but this woman hath anointed my
> feet with ointment. (Luke 7:37, 44)

The Pharisee saw his own thought. He did not see what the woman was doing and did not see what he had neglected to do. One can read this story as a commentary on how people see their own thought and do not see what others—women—are actually doing. Shifting the point of view from a male to a female perspective changes the way we think about the story. "She loved much" (Luke 7:47) is the story's refrain. Jesus' words to the woman are the teaching of peace. "Go in peace," he says to her (Luke 7:50).

More Women Ministers

Remembering that there were no chapters or verses in the Original Text, the story of the unnamed woman continues to what is now Luke 8.

> And it came to pass afterward, that he went throughout every
> city and village, preaching and shewing the glad tidings of the
> kingdom of God: and the twelve were with him, And certain

women, which had been healed of evil spirits and infirmities, Mary called Magdalene, out of whom went seven devils, And Joanna the wife of Chuza Herod's steward, and Susanna, and many others, which ministered unto him of their substance. (Luke 8:1–3).

In the face of biblical evidence, it hardly seems possible that there is even any lingering debate over whether women can be ministers. Perhaps the hitch is that Luke reported that Peter's mother-in-law ministered unto them (Luke 4:39); some read this to mean that ministering means a domestic duty.

Women Healed

Luke's stories about healings are woven together in significant ways. This is made startlingly clear in his recounting of the healing of a woman with an issue of blood "twelve years"—juxtaposed with the raising of the dead of "a twelve-year-old girl" (Luke 8:43–56). Implicit associations with menstruation and explicit statements calling both women "daughter" indicate Jesus' perception of these women as children of the Father-Mother God.

By his actions Jesus makes clear that the curse on Eve does not apply to any other woman—and that it is in the body that healing happens. Mark tells a story of a woman who suffered bleeding for years before Jesus healed her. "And straightway the fountain of her blood was dried up and she felt in her body that she was healed of that plague" (Mark 5:29).

So much has been said, thought, and done in the name of the Jesus of the Bible that the only sensible way to answer questions about who he is, is to read his biography in the Bible and decide for yourself.

John says, at the end of his Gospel,

Jesus did many other things as well. If every one of them were written down, I suppose that even the whole world

would not have room for the books that would be written.
(John 21:25 NIV)

But what is written in the Bible is certainly the place to start.

Sisters

Martha and Mary are sisters. And they are unlike. The differences
in their approaches to what is required by life may represent two
entirely separate schools of thought. If you have a sister, this
dichotomy may sound familiar. Luke 10:40 tells how "Martha was
cumbered about much serving," but the story, as told in chapters 11
and 12 of John, is a book in itself. The familiar story is one classic
place to practice critical reading of the Bible. As you study the story
of the sisters, you will see that it starts out, once more, with a man:
"a certain man was sick, named Lazarus of Bethany, the town of
Mary and her sister Martha" (John 11:1), then moves right away to
women.

The relationship of the women as sisters is mentioned, but it is
only in the next verse that we learn, parenthetically, that this certain man is their brother. Read on and you may think it strange that
six verses are spent sorting out relationships when, after all, this is
a story about the "who, what, when, where, and why" of resurrection. Thus, this set of identifications and balancing takes on shades
of meaning and varying hues.

Raising the Dead

Jesus is called and waits two days after he hears that Lazarus is sick.
He goes to Judea and finds that Lazarus has been in the grave four
days and many Jews are comforting Martha and Mary (John 11:19).
Martha rushes out upon Jesus' arrival; Mary sits still in the house.
Some women meet things head-on, questioning. Others wait quietly. Most women embrace one approach or the other at different
times in their lives.

Then said Martha unto Jesus, Lord, if thou hadst been
here, my brother had not died. But I know, that even now,
whatsoever thou wilt ask of God, God will give it thee.
Jesus saith unto her, Thy brother shall rise again.
Martha saith unto him, I know that he shall rise again in
the resurrection at the last day. (John 11:21–24)

Jesus challenges that theology:

Jesus said unto her, I am the resurrection, and the life: he
that believeth in me, though he were dead, yet shall he live:
And whosoever liveth and believeth in me shall never die.
Believest thou this? (John 11:25–26)

Martha identifies Jesus as the Christ:

She saith unto him, Yea, Lord: I believe that thou art the
Christ, the Son of God, which should come into the world.
(John 11:27)

Then Martha goes and calls her sister Mary and says that the
Teacher is asking for her. Mary gets up quickly and goes to Jesus,
falling at his feet, repeating what Martha said,

Lord, if thou hadst been here, my brother had not died.
When Jesus therefore saw her weeping, and the Jews also
weeping which came with her, he groaned in the spirit, and
was troubled, And said, Where have ye laid him? They said
unto him, Lord, come and see. Jesus wept. (John 11:32–35)

Moved and touched once more, Jesus orders the stone rolled
away from Lazarus' tomb.

Then they took away the stone from the place where the
dead was laid. And Jesus lifted up his eyes, and said, Father,

I thank thee that thou hast heard me. And I knew that thou
hearest me always: but because of the people which stand
by I said it, that they may believe that thou hast sent me.
(John 11:41–42)

Then Lazarus comes out of the grave, and Jesus says to the people, "Loose him and let him go" (John 11:44).

Mary of Bethany

It is significant that the Bible text says in the next verse: "many of
the Jews came to Mary and had seen the things which Jesus did"
(John 11:45). It is not Lazarus nor is it Martha to whom the Jews
come. They come to Mary.

The news of Lazarus' resurrection gets back to the Pharisees.
From that day forward, according to John, they plan Jesus' death.
Jesus, dwelling at the right hand of God, is nourished, until, with
the full knowledge there is a warrant out for his arrest and that his
crucifixion is near, he goes back to Bethany for the Passover.

There they made him a supper; and Martha served: but
Lazarus was one of them that sat at the table with him.
Then took Mary a pound of ointment of spikenard, very
costly, and anointed the feet of Jesus, and wiped his feet
with her hair: and the house was filled with the odour
of the ointment. (John 12:2–3)

Mark tells a similar story. It takes place in Bethany, but there is
no mention of Martha serving. There is an elaboration, however,
of the anointing of oil on the head by a woman—something that
one has before associated with a priest or the prophets. Judas questions whether the expensive oil is a waste of money that should
instead be given to the poor. Jesus says to leave Mary alone. He
says further:

She hath done what she could: she is come aforehand to anoint my body to the burying. Verily I say unto you, Wheresoever this gospel shall be preached throughout the whole world, this also that she hath done shall be spoken of for a memorial of her. (Mark 14:8–9)

Given all of this, the question is how much of the character of Martha or how much of Mary's one should strive for.

13

A Few Simple Rules

When Jesus heard it, he saith unto them, They that are whole have no need of the physician, but they that are sick . . .
—Mark 2:17

How do you get in touch with God? Prayer has long been an answer. Standing, sitting, kneeling? In a group or by yourself?

In early biblical narratives, before the establishment of any church or temple, people talk with Spirit, The Existing One, El Shaddai as readily as we now talk with each other. Some simply converse with God; Hannah prays silently; others lift up their eyes. When one does not know what to do, then at least one can start knowing what not to do. That is what the Bible does—alternating what not to do with what to do. All four Gospel writers report Jesus' instructions on how to pray. He begins with what not to do:

And then, when you pray, don't be like the play-actors. They love to stand and pray in the synagogues and at street-corners so that people may see them at it. But when you pray go into your own room, shut the door and pray to your Father privately. Your Father who sees all private things will reward you. For your Father knows your needs before you ask him. (Matthew 6:2–4 Phillips)

Father is defined in the Greek/English New Testament dictionary as "either the nearest ancestor: father of the corporeal nature, natural fathers, both parents." Another nonliteral translation of Father is "nourisher, protector, upholder, creator, preserver, guardian of spiritual beings." Apparently, substituting any or all of those words in place of Father does not change the spiritual sense of the following prayer—as Bobby McFerrin has done in his translation of the Twenty-third Psalm (see Chapter Eight of this book).

The Only Prayer

What is now called the Lord's Prayer reads as follows in Matthew 6:9–13:

> After this manner therefore pray ye: Our Father which art in heaven, Hallowed be thy name.
> Thy kingdom come. Thy will be done in earth, as it is in heaven.
> Give us this day our daily bread.
> And forgive us our debts, as we forgive our debtors.
> And lead us not into temptation, but deliver us from evil: For thine is the kingdom and the power, and the glory, for ever. Amen.

Comparing Luke's record of the Lord's Prayer with Matthew's, just in the King James Version translation, is a simple way to see the differences in one central biblical idea. Not only is there no "Amen" in Luke's version of the Lord's Prayer, but even the same translators of the King James Version have translated the prayer differently in Matthew and Luke.

> Lord, teach us to pray, as John also taught his disciples.
> And he said unto them, When ye pray, say, Our Father which art in heaven, Hallowed be thy name. Thy kingdom come. Thy will be done, as in heaven, so in earth. Give us day by day our daily bread.
> And forgive us our sins; for we also forgive every one that is indebted to us. And lead us not into temptation; but deliver us from evil. (Luke 11:1–4)

Test of Prayer

In Luke's version the test of prayer is set in the context of friendship and family and healing. In Jesus' words in the verses that follow there is reference to "three loaves"—an echo of "the leaven the women hid in three measures of meal" which relates to the "kingdom of heaven" in the thirteenth chapters of both Matthew and Luke.

That kingdom of heaven was created in Genesis 1 by the moving on the waters of *ruah Elohim*, not by an angry male God who is only going to allow a few inside His gates. For those interested in a journey on a profound path filled with intricate allusion, an inquiry into women's relation to three measures, bread, and meal is a fascinating road to walk. Remember to start with Sarah and the time she made loaves with three measures for the three men who came unexpectedly to visit.

> And he said unto them, Which of you shall have a friend, and shall go unto him at midnight, and say unto him, Friend, lend me three loaves;
>
> For a friend of mine in his journey is come to me, and I have nothing to set before him?
>
> And he from within shall answer and say, Trouble me not: the door is now shut, and my children are with me in bed; I cannot rise and give thee.
>
> I say unto you, Though he will not rise and give him, because he is his friend, yet because of his importunity he will rise and give him as many as he needeth.
>
> And I say unto you, Ask, and it shall be given you; seek, and ye shall find; knock, and it shall be opened unto you.
>
> For every one that asketh receiveth; and he that seeketh findeth; and to him that knocketh it shall be opened.
>
> If a son shall ask bread of any of you that is a father, will he give him a stone? or if he ask a fish, will he for a fish give him a serpent?

Or if he shall ask an egg, will he offer him a scorpion?

If ye then, being evil, know how to give good gifts unto your children: how much more shall your heavenly Father give the Holy Spirit to them that ask him? (Luke 11:5–13)

Ask and Receive

Matthew gives a specific, illustrative example of prayer. A woman of Canaan, a foreigner and not a Jew, thinks she needs an intercessor when she goes to Jesus and says: "Have mercy on me O Lord, thou son of David, my daughter is grievously vexed with a devil" (Matthew 15:22). Jesus does not answer her. She does not go away moping or weeping. She drives his disciples to distraction. She is so annoying that they go to Jesus and ask him to send her away. He still has not answered the woman. His answer to the disciples is cryptic: "I am not sent but unto the lost sheep of the house of Israel" (Matthew 15:24).

The woman persists.

"Then came she and worshipped him, saying, Lord help me." Jesus may seem cruel and heartless when he answers, "It is not meet to take the children's bread, and to cast it to dogs" (Matthew 15:25–26).

Her answer is direct and to the point: "Truth, Lord. yet the dogs eat of the crumbs which fall from their master's table."

Jesus replies, "O woman, great is thy faith; be it unto thee even as thou wilt. And her daughter was made whole from that very hour" (Matthew 15:27–28).

The woman with the confidence to speak truth to Jesus finds that it is in her power to get what she asks for. It takes persistence. She comes away with not just a one-time healing but also the knowledge that her desire for her daughter's return to wholeness is in itself a prayer.

It seems difficult to grasp that healing can happen in an instant or at a distance. But as the Spirit of the Creation appears simultaneously throughout the universe and beyond, this is not outside the boundaries of possibility and the biblical text. Many today report such healings.

There is little question that the Bible is concerned with the care, feeding, wellness, and understanding of the body. It is for the body that we focus our need and desire for healing. In the light of that need, perhaps we should examine more closely what our own bodies are and who and what controls them. Asking for this information, the Bible says, is the way to get it.

Trouble the Judge

But what if the healing doesn't come? Or what if we are not getting what we really need to live? Again, this time in the Gospel of Luke, a woman's story suggests an answer:

> And he spake a parable unto them to this end, that men ought always to pray, and not to faint; Saying, There was in a city a judge, which feared not God neither regarded man: And there was a widow in that city; and she came unto him, saying, Avenge me of mine adversary. And he would not for a while: but afterward he said within himself, Though I fear not God, nor regard man;
> Yet because this widow troubleth me, I will avenge her, lest by her continual coming she weary me. (Luke 18:1–5)

The woman in this parable is the prototypical person who needs help in a world that devalues the woman "alone." The Bible, however, says that the widow, the woman alone—literally, metaphorically, physically, or emotionally—is vindicated through her persistent need and prayer. Persistence and prayer in this context means figuring out not only what you need but also what is standing in the way of getting what you need.

The Bible says to women: challenge fear. Challenge the idea that you cannot do something for yourself. Challenge every thought that says you don't deserve healing, or good, or all that makes up an abundant life. Don't give up, this parable says. God makes provision for you.

Beatitudes

There is much more in the Bible about provision than there is about punishment, much more about love and humility than there is about anger and pride. Jesus looks back into the Scriptures to a "broken and contrite heart," "meekness," and "mourning" (first introduced in the Bible when Abraham mourned for Sarah), and he echoes biblical precepts now referred to as the Beatitudes. Matthew describes the scene:

> And his fame went throughout all Syria: and they brought unto him all sick people that were taken with divers diseases and torments, and those which were possessed with devils, and those which were lunatic, and those that had the palsy; and he healed them.
>
> And there followed him great multitudes of people from Galilee, and from Decapolis, and from Jerusalem, and from Judaea, and from beyond Jordan.
>
> And seeing the multitudes, he went up into a mountain: and when he was set, his disciples came unto him: And he opened his mouth, and taught them, saying,
>
> Blessed are the poor in spirit: for theirs is the kingdom of heaven.
>
> Blessed are they that mourn: for they shall be comforted.
>
> Blessed are the meek: for they shall inherit the earth.
>
> Blessed are they which do hunger and thirst after righteousness: for they shall be filled.
>
> Blessed are the merciful: for they shall obtain mercy.
>
> Blessed are the pure in heart: for they shall see God.
>
> Blessed are the peacemakers: for they shall be called the children of God.

Blessed are they which are persecuted for righteousness' sake: for theirs is the kingdom of heaven.

Blessed are ye, when men shall revile you, and persecute you, and shall say all manner of evil against you falsely, for my sake.

Rejoice, and be exceeding glad: for great is your reward in heaven: for so persecuted they the prophets which were before you. (Matthew 4:24–5:12)

The God of the Bible is not an angry man—though some still see this outdated notion. It's worth your while to search the Hebrew Bible and find the places where the Beatitudes first appear. You might start by looking back to the reference to Moses as being meek. This is another starting point to seeing the Bible as the non-denominational story of the spiritual self. Illustrating, through the texts, that God is not terrifying nor confined to national or denominational interpretations may do more good for ensuing generations and the teaching of peace than we can know.

The Golden Rule

If there is one thing almost universally agreed upon about the Bible, it is that it says, "Do unto others as you would have them do unto you." Jesus, when asked what is the greatest commandment, sums it up this way in the King James translation:

Master, which is the great commandment in the law?
Jesus said unto him, Thou shalt love the Lord thy God with all thy heart, and with all thy soul, and with all thy mind.

This is the first and great commandment.

And the second is like unto it, Thou shalt love thy neighbour as thyself.

On these two commandments hang all the law and the prophets. (Matthew 22:37–40)

The mandate to love thy neighbor is called the Golden Rule. Looking for all the biblical precursors to Jesus' statement and following this trail acquaints us with the law and prophets of the Hebrew Bible as well as many more of Jesus' thoughts. As you follow this trail you will not be trapped in the tangles of theology. Instead, you will travel through the wilderness with Moses and hear the Voice's reminder in Deuteronomy 10:19 that "ye were strangers in the land of Egypt." Instead of tangled theology and mistaken views of women, you will be in the way with Abigail, preparing meal and bread with Sarah, at the well with Rachel.

You will find yourself at the marriage feast at Cana where the water is changed to wine. You will drink of the inspiration that comes with seeing women in the Bible not as chattel living in bad times but as daughters of One God, Spirit, *ruah Elohim*, who is nourisher, protector, upholder, Creator, preserver, guardian.

14

Who Tells the Story?

It was Mary Magdalene, and Joanna, and Mary the mother of James, and other women that were with them, which told these things unto the apostles. And their words seemed to them as idle tales, and they believed them not.

—Luke 24:10–11

Have we ever challenged the assumption that men were the only sources for the Gospel accounts of Jesus' life? We should, as in some places the accounts could only have come from women. And not surprisingly, those accounts focus on relationships. Matthew, Mark, and Luke say that Jesus began his ministry preaching in Galilee or a synagogue (Matthew 4:17, Mark 1:4, Luke 4:15). John begins his account of Jesus' ministry at a wedding.

All of John must be read to realize the full import of the nature and message of Jesus of Nazareth. Biblically, what has gone before and everything that is to come is alluded to by the ideas and words John uses in his Gospel. The first sentence in John echoes the first chapter of Genesis and then on into Revelation—particularly the last chapter of that book. The first words of John and the first words of the entire Bible are "In the beginning." In the beginning is synchronous time, with all things made by God and with life as light shining in the darkness. "In him was life; and the life was the light of men. And the light shineth in darkness; and the darkness comprehended it not" (John 1:4–5).

Self-Referential Text

John's Gospel says Elisabeth's son, John the Baptist, sent from God "was not that Light but was sent to bear witness of that Light" (John

1:8). Looking at each verse of John is a reminder of what has come before in the Bible. For example, verse 29 says that the Baptist sees Jesus and calls him the "Lamb of God." We remember Abraham and his near-sacrifice; we recall Abraham's statement: "God himself will provide the lamb for the burnt offering . . ." (Genesis 22:8). The Baptist sees the "Spirit descending from heaven like a dove" (John 1:32). This echoes the *ruah Elohim*, the Spirit of God, and the dove that Noah sends out from the ark after the flood to see if it is time to come to dry land in Genesis 8:8. The phrase "Spirit descending from heaven like a dove" echoes the second and fifth days of the Creation described in the first chapter of Genesis.

The day after his vision, the Baptist sees Jesus pass by and says, "Behold, the Lamb of God" (John 1:36). Two of the Baptist's disciples then follow Jesus, who turns and asks them, "What seek ye?"

"Where dwellest thou?" they ask him in return (John 1:38).

God has already asked Job a similar question: "Where is the way where light dwelleth?" (Job 38:19). In John 1:39 Jesus answers the two disciples: "Come and see. They came and saw where he dwelt, and abode with him that day."

Where the Light Dwells

Where did Jesus dwell? What did they see? What day? When they return and say to others that they had "found the Messias, which is, being interpreted, the Christ" (John 1:41), do we imagine that he took them to some house, somewhere in some town in the Middle East, and that they spent a day there?

Andrew is one of the men who sees where "the Light dwells." He goes and finds his brother Simon Peter and brings him to Jesus, who, on seeing him, calls him "Simon, the son of Jona"—a reference to Jonah, who spent three days in the belly of the whale and who, against his desires, preached to Nineveh and saved that whole city (Jonah 1:1–4:11).

Jesus then tells Simon that in the future "Thou shalt be called Cephas, which is by interpretation, a stone." Peter and Cephas both carry the meaning "rock" or "stone." The Baptist has said in Luke 3:8, "God is able of these stones to raise up children to Abraham."

Reflecting on John's Gospel takes the reader to the parallel texts in Genesis 1. "In the beginning" puts John's Gospel on the same track as the unfolding days of spiritual Creation. The first day mentioned in John's Gospel is that day that the disciples saw where Jesus dwelt and that day in Genesis on which the "Spirit moved on the face of the waters." The second day mentioned is the day following, on which *ruah Elohim* said there is a firmament to divide the waters in two. The third day of spiritual Creation pairs with the next account from John: "And the third day there was a marriage in Cana of Galilee" (John 2:1). We are in the third day at the wedding—both in John's process of revealing the story and in the literal words. The story is set in the dimension of the third day of Genesis, on which "the seed was in itself."

The Bridegroom

> And the third day there was a marriage in Cana of Galilee; and the mother of Jesus was there: And both Jesus was called, and his disciples, to the marriage.
>
> And when they wanted wine, the mother of Jesus saith unto him, They have no wine. Jesus saith unto her, Woman, what have I to do with thee? mine hour is not yet come. His mother saith unto the servants, Whatsoever he saith unto you, do it. (John 2:1–5)

Mary may well be the source for John's story. John himself could have been at the wedding.

Reading the Bible can take one out of the everyday, and if we are out of the everyday at the wedding (though there is certainly that element to the account), we look at the active participation of the mother of Jesus. She knows and the reader knows that her child was conceived spiritually. The feast has run out of wine. The wedding ceremony unites male and female. Jesus, at his mother's bidding, asks for the "waterpots." He will turn water into wine. Filling the waterpots with water is not only literal but also echoes the Spirit that moved on the face of the waters.

Water is the essential element of Creation. Wine can refer to inspiration. Changing the water into wine, as Jesus does, is not merely a parlor trick. John's account may be read that a more spiritual sense of Creation—of the union of male and female—is to take place at a very traditional, very human wedding. When the governor of the feast tastes the water made wine, he calls the bridegroom. Who is the bridegroom? John 3:29 has the Baptist comparing himself to the friend of the bridegroom. Do we simply assume that the bridegroom is the man being married that third day at Cana? What are other possible implications? Certainly the other nearly two dozen references to "bridegroom" are messianic, metaphorical, proverbial, or taken to be references to Jesus. Isaiah 62:5 has the bridegroom rejoicing over the bride.

The texts are building to Revelation 21:2, in which the Holy City is adorned as a "bride for her husband."

The Christ

After the good wine at the wedding, Jesus and his whole family go down to Capernaum, and there are not too many days before it is Passover and Jesus goes up to Jerusalem. There he whips money-changers out of the temple, speaks of "the temple of his body" and says that man must be "born of water and of the Spirit" (John 2:21, 3:5). This is often taken literally and can certainly mean that man must be born again into the male and female of the Creation out of water by the Spirit, *ruah Elohim*, in the first chapter of Genesis.

Women continue to hold center stage along with Jesus in the fourth chapter of John. The Baptist is still baptizing, and there is water everywhere. Jesus asks for a drink. The physical setting is, John says, at the site of Jacob's well. The background may be the well, but the conscious revelation of spiritual identity is the foreground. A Samaritan woman comes to draw water.

Jesus says: "Give me to drink" (John 4:7).

Then saith the woman of Samaria unto him, How is it that thou, being a Jew, askest drink of me, which am a woman of Samaria? for the Jews have no dealings with the Samaritans. Jesus answered and said unto her, If thou knewest the gift of God, and who it is that saith to thee, Give me to drink; thou wouldest have asked of him, and he would have given thee living water.

The woman saith unto him, Sir, thou hast nothing to draw with, and the well is deep: from whence then hast thou that living water? (John 4:9–11)

That Jesus sees beyond gender or tribal distinctions is often noted when describing his character. But readers bearing in mind the significance that water plays in the rest of the Bible will draw deeper meaning from the exchange between the woman and Jesus. Readers have noted that Martha and this woman of Samaria recognize the Christ as do Peter and Matthew in the opening of his Gospel.

There are references to a lack of a husband; in fact, Jesus tells the woman she has had five husbands. The woman's perception is that Jesus is a prophet. In this exchange Jesus says, "God is a Spirit: and they that worship him must worship him in Spirit and in truth" (John 4:24). Here again the translators of the King James Version have inserted "him" for God when the actual Greek word used in the Original Text is *pneu'ma*, a noun with no gender or neutral gender, which refers to the "breath, wind, Spirit" that moved on the face of the waters in Genesis 1.

Two People at the Well

There were only two people at the well—the unnamed woman of Samaria and Jesus. Who reported this encounter to John? The woman does leave her waterpot and tells the men in the city to

"Come, see a man, which told me all things that ever I did: is not this the Christ?" (John 4:29). "Come, see," she said, using the words Jesus used to the two disciples who wanted to know where he dwelt. And they came. There is no hesitation. The woman is believed, and the men do what she says to do.

The men listen to Jesus, and the woman hears from them that it is no longer because of her statement alone that they believe Jesus is the Christ. They tell her they believe it "not because of thy saying: for we have heard him for ourselves, and know that this is indeed the Christ, the Saviour of the world" (John 4:42). Sad to say, some biblical accounts report that men don't believe women, as we shall see after the Resurrection. Would it matter if men heard the news from another man? Is it that one has to hear and see for oneself?

Mary, Mary, Mary

John's recounting of the infamous story of the woman taken in adultery in John verses 8:3–11 points clearly to the fact that sin is not merely an act but what you think about the act, or even what you think. Jesus says, "He that is without sin among you, let him first cast a stone at her" (John 8:7). Each man, convicted by his own conscience, stops throwing stones, and one by one, the oldest first, they depart, leaving the woman alone with Jesus. There is no one left to accuse the woman of sin or to stone her. Only Jesus or the woman could have told the end of this story.

Who Is the Woman?

The woman in this story is unnamed. Again, she could be any of us. There is no reference in the story to confirm that the woman is Mary Magdalene. It is a puzzle, still, how Mary Magdalene's name became associated with adultery or why she has been called a whore. Using a concordance to search the Scriptures for references to Mary of Magdala or Mary Magdalene, one sees for oneself how simple it is to clear up misconceptions—even those held for two thousand years. It is not as romantic, perhaps, as it is to read speculation on who Mary Magdalene was or what her relationship to Jesus was, but it does make plain the biblical facts about her.

One fact is clear: Mary Magdalene—alone or with a handful of other women, depending on whether one reads Matthew, Mark, Luke, or John—reported the Resurrection of Jesus Christ.

But there can be no Resurrection without the crucifixion.

Crucifixion

Jesus describes his impending crucifixion this way: "A woman when she is in travail hath sorrow, because her hour is come; but as soon as she is delivered of the child, she remembereth no more the anguish, for joy that a man is born into the world" (John 16:21). We will see the woman in travail again in Revelation.

The particulars of the crucifixion are well known. There is a Passover Supper where Jesus breaks bread and there is wine (Matthew, Mark, and Luke), and Jesus washes the disciples' feet as the unnamed woman and Mary Magdala washed his. Jesus prays in the garden of Gethsemane, enjoining his disciples to "pray that ye enter not into temptation" (Luke 22:40). Here Jesus prays to let the Father's will—"thy will," not his—be done (Matthew 26:42). It's fair to say that Jesus lives the Lord's Prayer—his own prayer— moment by moment.

Judas identifies Jesus to the chief priests and elders of the people. Jesus appears before them and all the council; Peter, as foretold by Jesus, denies his Master. Jesus is brought before Pilate. Judas dies. Pilate questions Jesus. Jesus is sentenced to die, and they lead him away to crucify him (Matthew 26:57–27:31).

The account of the crucifixion as found in Matthew, chapter 27, ends with

And many women were there beholding afar off, which followed Jesus from Galilee, ministering unto him: among which was Mary Magdalene, and Mary the mother of James and Joses, and the mother of Zebedee's children.

Mark's account is in chapters 14 and 15:

There were also women looking on afar off: among whom was Mary Magdalene, and Mary the mother of James the less and of Joses, and Salome; (who also when he was in Galilee, followed him and ministered unto him;) and many other women which came up with him unto Jerusalem.

Luke says in chapter 23:

And as they led him away, they laid hold upon one Simon, a Cyrenian, coming out of the country, and on him they laid the cross, that he might bear it after Jesus. And there followed him a great company of people, and of women, which also bewailed and lamented him. But Jesus turning unto them said, Daughters of Jerusalem, weep not for me, but weep for yourselves, and for your children.

John 19:25–28 gives this account:

Now there stood by the cross of Jesus his mother, and his mother's sister, Mary the wife of Cleophas, and Mary Magdalene. When Jesus therefore saw his mother, and the disciple standing by, whom he loved, he saith unto his mother, Woman, behold thy son!
    Then saith he to the disciple, Behold thy mother! And from that hour that disciple took her unto his own home. After this, Jesus knowing that all things were now accomplished, that the scripture might be fulfilled, saith, I thirst.

All four Gospel writers say that on the first day of the week Mary Magdalene was at the tomb. Attempting to determine if that day is Saturday, Sunday, or Monday may be missing the point. The reference could well be to the first day of Creation when *ruah Elohim* moves on the face of the waters. Mary's story—what she saw, heard, felt, and did—will lead you to the scene. Through her experience the Bible reader is given a glimpse of the Resurrection encounter. Through her experience you can follow for yourself how it dawns on her what is going on and that she is witness, one who carries the report to the disciples. And if she is the only witness, then only she or Jesus could have reported the event.

Luke says that Mary Magdalene—along with Joanna and Mary, the mother of James—reported to the apostles that they had seen two angels who told them, "he . . . is risen" (Luke 24:6). And, Luke says, "Their words seem to them as idle tales, and they believed them not" (24:11).

Until the men see and hear for themselves, they do not believe. Jesus, whom they don't recognize, walks with two of the disciples on the road to Emmaus.

"And beginning at Moses and all the prophets, he expounded unto them in all the scriptures the things concerning himself" (Luke 24:27). Then, they recognize him.

15

Spreading the Word

> And I intreat thee also, true yokefellow, help those women which
> laboured with me in the gospel, with Clement also, and with
> other my fellow labourers, whose names are in the book of life.
> —Philippians 4:3

Have you ever wondered just exactly *who* or *what* the Holy
Ghost is?

Mary, the mother of Jesus, in the first recorded meeting of what
was to become the Christian church, met together with about 120
women and men who were disciples of her son (Acts 1:14). The
people at this meeting included those who had seen Jesus and
talked with him for forty days after the crucifixion.

The Book of Acts, Luke's account of what happened at this first
organizational meeting of the Christian church, is, as is his Gospel,
addressed to Theophilus—friend of God (Acts 1:1). Those who
count themselves friends of God find the Gospel and the Book of
Acts to be addressed to them.

The Ascension, or disappearance of Jesus from human sight, is
reported in Acts 1:6–11. Jesus is taken up in a cloud. This is perhaps
a reference to the cloud that Moses was in for forty days and nights,
the cloud that the Israelites followed on their travels to the Promised
Land. Much of Acts is interwoven with texts from Exodus.

The Crucifixion, Resurrection, and Ascension are such singular and extraordinary events that one wonders how there could be
anything worth reporting after them. But just after the Ascension,
as Luke reports, there is an issue at hand: to replace the dead Judas
with another disciple. This is done. There is prayer to know what
the Lord wanted and then a vote, by which Matthais is elected.

And there appeared unto them cloven tongues like as of fire, and it sat upon each of them. And they were all filled with the Holy Ghost, and began to speak with other tongues, as the Spirit gave them utterance. (Acts 2:3–4)

No Translator Needed

The human form of Jesus is not seen, but the presence of the Holy Ghost, the Spirit, comes to each woman and man in the house. This event is called the Day of Pentecost.

In this meeting there is no disputation over theology. No separation of one group from another. The men don't gather in one part of the room and the women in another. They all speak in their own languages, but every man heard them speak in his own language (Acts 2:6).

Greeks, Egyptians, Persians all hear the speaking as if it is in their native tongue, but the people who are speaking in the Spirit were Galileans. Such is the effect of the Holy Ghost—the language of Spirit communicates without regard to nationality. Jesus had promised this in John 15 and 16, and it happens.

There are eighty-nine references in the New Testament and Gospels to the Holy Ghost—nearly half in the Book of Acts. The first reference is in Matthew 1:18: it is the Holy Ghost that fills Mary's womb with Jesus. The second-to-last reference is in the First Letter of John: "The Father, the Word, and the Holy Ghost: and these three are one."

Have we not all one Father? Hath not one God created us? (Malachi 2:10)

In the beginning was the Word, and the Word was with God, and the Word was God." (John 1:1)

Hear O Israel; The Lord our God is one Lord. (Deuteronomy 6:4)

These sample texts indicate that each and every time the word *Father, Word,* or *Holy Ghost* appears, it is One. Distinct in office but One. The Holy Ghost and Spirit are often used interchangeably. One definition of Holy Ghost is: "a spirit, i.e., a simple essence, devoid of all or at least all grosser matter, and possessed of the power of knowing, desiring, deciding, and acting." Another is: "a movement of air (a gentle blast) of the wind, hence the wind itself" (KJV, New Testament Greek Lexicon).

The Spirit Spreads

The new young church is organized economically so that all are one in financial resources. All throw in what they have and then the money and property are redistributed. The focus moves away from the human form of Jesus; the presence of the Holy Spirit is available to all. In Acts, Luke reports healing after healing by the disciples as they live in the afterglow of the Resurrection, Ascension, and influx of the Holy Spirit. Again, Luke reports of healing of both men and women—saints and widows being of equal weight.

> And it came to pass, as Peter passed throughout all quarters, he came down also to the saints which dwelt at Lydda. And there he found a certain man named Aeneas, which had kept his bed eight years, and was sick of the palsy. And Peter said unto him, Aeneas, Jesus Christ maketh thee whole: arise, and make thy bed. And he arose immediately. And all that dwelt at Lydda and Saron saw him, and turned to the Lord.
>
> Now there was at Joppa a certain disciple named Tabitha, which by interpretation is called Dorcas: this woman was full of good works and almsdeeds which she did. And it came to pass in those days, that she was sick, and died: whom when they had washed, they laid her in an upper chamber. And forasmuch as Lydda was nigh to Joppa, and the disciples had

heard that Peter was there, they sent unto him two men, desiring him that he would not delay to come to them.

Then Peter arose and went with them. When he was come, they brought him into the upper chamber: and all the widows stood by him weeping, and shewing the coats and garments which Dorcas made, while she was with them.

But Peter put them all forth, and kneeled down, and prayed; and turning him to the body said, Tabitha, arise. And she opened her eyes: and when she saw Peter, she sat up. And he gave her his hand, and lifted her up, and when he had called the saints and widows, presented her alive. (Acts 9:32–41)

One of the disciples, Philip, is transported instantly to and from a watering spot where he and an Ethiopian Jew read the Book of Isaiah in the light of the life of Jesus Christ. There are martyrs stoned to death, there is great turmoil among Jews and Gentiles, and more people begin to believe the gospel of the eyewitnesses. One example is the encounter between Philip and the Ethiopian (Acts 8:26–40).

And at that time there was great persecution against the church which was at Jerusalem . . . as for Saul, he made havock of the church, entering into every house, and haling men and women and committed them to prison. (Acts 8:1, 3)

Saul of Tarsus is on the rampage—"breathing out threatenings and slaughter against the disciples of the Lord" (Acts 9:1). He is on his way to Damascus to capture and torture disciples of Jesus. A light shines on him; he falls to the earth and hears a voice. The speaker identifies himself as Jesus, who tells him to go on into the city where he will be told what to do next. When Saul gets up from the earth, he is blind.

In Damascus, his sight is restored by Ananias who has also heard the voice of Jesus telling him to search out this man who is so feared by Christians (Acts 9:1–18). Saul (later known as Paul once his sight is restored; Acts 13:9) tells his story again and again and again. As Gabriel Josipivici says in the chapter "St. Paul and Subjectivity" in his *The Book of God: A Response to the Bible* (1988), "It would be absurd to ask which came first for Paul, the message or the impulse toward personal witness, for each clearly reinforces the other" (p. 240). Josipivici also makes the point that "no two commentators have ever agreed on what he is saying" (p. 240). Josipivici notes that Augustine follows Paul in the self-dramatized autobiographical mode.

Paul and His Impact

Paul, the converted Pharisee, formerly Saul, eloquent and impassioned letter writer, missionary of the Christ, is translated by men and condensed into sound bites that say a handful of things that have caused many women severe pain through the ages. Paul's words are used to dominate women and to subvert the message of Jesus Christ and the Bible. Some women have a violent reaction to even the mention of his name. Others say that to question him is heresy.

The Letter Writer

What Paul did to anger so many is to write letters that are still read today. Letters from five men—or six men, if one counts Luke and the Book of Acts—form the bulk of the New Testament. Paul, Peter, John, James, and Jude wrote letters to friends and churches while they traveled, preaching and healing. If you are one of those people who still write letters, you will appreciate that good ones are not easy to write and not often enough received.

In the King James Version, Paul begins a letter—chapter 16 of what is now the Book of Romans—by referencing the women and men in the cause. (Presumably the Phebe he commends carries this letter on her person.)

I commend unto you Phebe our sister, which is a servant of the church which is at Cenchrea: That ye receive her in the Lord, as becometh saints, and that ye assist her in whatsoever business she hath need of you: for she hath been a succourer of many, and of myself also. Greet Priscilla and Aquila my helpers in Christ Jesus: Who have for my life laid down their own necks: unto whom not only I give thanks, but also all the churches of the Gentiles. Likewise greet the church that is in their house. Salute my wellbeloved Epaenetus, who is the firstfruits of Achaia unto Christ. Greet Mary, who bestowed much labour on us. Salute Andronicus and Junia, my kinsmen, and my fellowprisoners, who are of note among the apostles, who also were in Christ before me. (Romans 16:1–7)

The Bible for Today's Family: Contemporary English Version translates the first part of that passage as follows:

I have good things to say about Phoebe, who is a leader in the church at Cenchrae. Welcome her in a way that is proper for someone who has faith in the Lord and is one of God's own people. Help her in any way you can. After all, she has proved to be a respected leader for many others, including me.

Paul goes on to send greetings to many women and men; in fact, all but seven verses out of the entire letter are personal messages to friends. Paul's closing words to Timothy in another letter are "When you come, bring the coat I left at Troas with Carpus. Don't forget to bring the scrolls, especially the ones made of leather." He signs off: "Do your best to come before winter" (2 Timothy 4:13–21 CEV).

Paul Ponders

It is clear that Paul was a man before he was so widely known as a saint. But merely recognizing the personal nature of some of Paul's concerns or his respect and acknowledgment of women as leaders in the church does not dismiss the impact of some interpretations or translations of other sayings attributed to him. For example, Paul seems to speak literally and in only one dimension when he says that women must wear coverings on their heads in church while praying and prophesying. In this mention in 1 Corinthians 11:5, Paul's words seem to be a comment on the second creation—Adam and Eve. He likens an uncovered head to one that is shaven. Remember Hannah and her son Samuel and her promise to not shave his head? The biblical covered or unshaven head is a sign of commitment to The Existing One.

Despite that, Paul says, "Judge in yourselves" (1 Corinthians 11:13). Better to judge for yourself than to get into an argument, he seems to be saying. To some, the rest of this letter of Paul seems concerned only with whether you've eaten or drunk before you come to church. To others, the letter is instruction in spiritually diagnosing one's body through Christ. The range of readings of Paul is extreme.

There is the wonderful and familiar: "Though I speak with the tongues of men and of angels, and have not charity, I am become as sounding brass, or a tinkling cymbal" (1 Corinthians 13:1). And then Paul cuts back to prophecy: "Follow the way of love and eagerly desire spiritual gifts, especially the gift of prophecy. . . . He who speaks in a tongue edifies himself, but he who prophecies edifies the church" (1 Corinthians 14:1, 4 NIV).

Here and in the other places in which Paul speaks about prophecy, women are included. And, then just when you thought it was safe to go back into the waters:

> Let your women keep silence in the churches: for it is not
> permitted unto them to speak; but they are commanded to
> be under obedience, as also saith the law. And if they will
> learn any thing, let them ask their husbands at home: for it
> is a shame for women to speak in the church. (1 Corinthians
> 14:34–35)

The passage just quoted is preceded by: "For God is not the author of confusion, but of peace, as in all churches of the saints" (1 Corinthians 14:33). Some scholars believe that this text is a "scriptural gloss," meaning other people have altered Paul's words. But that won't really do for those who take each word of the Bible literally and who also believe all Scripture to be from God. Fortunately, the Bible also says that women in the churches may prophesy and that each reader discovers the text for herself.

Paul's Dilemmas

We can say that Paul had dazzling bursts of clarity when the mist thinned—and we can say there were times when he just didn't get it. We can say that this or that text is inconsistent with Paul's other practices and professions on women and equality. We can say many things. What is certain, though, is that Paul commented both on spiritual Creation and on Adam and Eve.

Even Paul said he didn't get it all.

> Brethren, I count not myself to have apprehended: but this
> one thing I do, forgetting those things which are behind,
> and reaching forth unto those things which are before,
> I press toward the mark for the prize of the high calling
> of God in Christ Jesus. (Philippians 3:13–14)

There are more references in the Bible to women prophesying than there are to women being silent. Acts 2:17–18 is one, offering a fascinating but brief glimpse of what must have been an intriguing household: "Leaving the next day, we reached Caesarea and stayed at the house of Philip the evangelist, one of the Seven. He had four unmarried daughters who prophesied" (Acts 21:8–9 NIV).

There are, too, the words of King Lemuel, "the prophecy that his mother taught him" (Proverbs 31:1). This last verse prefaces the poem long used in religious tradition to describe the ideal woman: Proverbs 31:10–31. It's a not-to-be-missed antidote to any feelings that being a woman keeps one circumscribed, which begins: "Who can find a virtuous woman, for her price is above rubies."

Paul knew Scripture as few did and must have been familiar with this, one of the best-known passages in the Hebrew Bible. Because he was preaching a message of fulfillment of Scripture, and Proverbs 31:10–31 puts no limitation on women, Paul might have been in conflict over what to say to squabbling congregations.

Wives and Husbands

"Wives, submit yourself unto your own husbands, as unto the Lord," Paul says in a letter to the Ephesians 5:22. Before newer readings, in the days when "Lord" was understood as meaning a male God and not Spirit, this out-of-context statement of Paul's led to male domination of women. But looking at the whole of Ephesians chapters 5 and 6, we see how everyone—husbands and wives—is to act in the context of the equality of all relations that Paul discusses there. Paul says it is "all a great mystery [of] Christ and the church" ("church" in biblical Greek is *ekklesia*: like "Israel," a feminine word).

Paul sets his reflections on the relation of Christ and the church in the context of two earlier biblical statements. One is the statement in Genesis 2:24: "Therefore shall a man leave his father and his mother, and shall cleave unto his wife; and they shall be one flesh." In his Letter to the Ephesians, Paul too is talking about the spiritual union of male and female in Genesis 1:27.

If chapters 5 and 6 of Paul's Letter to the Ephesians are read in the light of the first two chapters of Genesis, then it is clear that what Paul is talking about is a "great mystery concerning the church"—not merely literal marriage. Another word for mystery is *paradox*—a seeming contradiction.

Peter Too

There is little question that those who wrote the history of the church have interpreted some parts of the letters that were written to one person or a group at one time and pronounced that they should be the last word throughout eternity. So what are we to do about the seeming inconsistencies between Paul and Peter? Peter says nobody with aspirations to an office in the church should drink wine, whereas Paul, in a letter to Timothy, suggests that Timothy "drink some wine for the stomach and other infirmities you have."

Inconsistencies force the reader to acknowledge, at the very least, that even men deemed by other men to be saints still were men with past histories and in the midst of their own contemporary mores. Each of us is an individual at different states and stages of progress. But as the full and complete idea of who you are as God made you is already established, says the Bible, there is no reason to fear growth or change. Paul knew Scripture, and as Habakkuk 2:14 says, sooner or later "the earth shall be filled with the knowledge of the glory of the Lord, as the waters cover the sea"—the whole earth will acknowledge spiritual Creation.

Paul also sees the impartial and universal nature of spiritual Creation when he says, "There is neither Jew nor Greek, there is neither bond nor free, there is neither male or female; for ye are all one in Christ Jesus" (Galatians 3:28). There are no inconsistencies between Peter and Paul in their addressing of both the first and second accounts of Creation.

More Mail; Plain Places

Though Paul waxes eloquent in so many of his compelling New Testament letters, John's three small letters should also be read. The first letter of John is a description of love. "God is Love," John says in 1 John 4:8. We can't ask for more. John's first letter is also a description of the children of light. The second letter is written to a woman, "the elect lady and her children." The historically minded might wonder who this woman is. As John has been called mystical, the mystically minded may wonder if this is one of those occasions of prophetic biblical time and deduce that the letter speaks not to one who got her mail in a desert town, but perhaps to the woman to come in Revelation described later by John.

Looking Back and Ahead

The last letter of the New Testament is Jude's. He reminds us of Jesus Christ, God, Father, mercy, peace, love, faith, The Existing One, the people saved out of the land of Egypt, angels, Sodom and Gomorrah, Michael the archangel, Moses, Cain, Enoch, Adam, Holy Ghost, eternal life, compassion, and making a difference. And before we get to the final conflict and resolution of the Bible, Jude says,

> Now unto him that is able to keep you from falling, and to present you faultless before the presence of his glory with exceeding joy, to the only wise God our Saviour; be glory and majesty, dominion and power, both now and ever. Amen. (Jude 1:24–25)

16

The Spirit and the Bride

And the woman which thou sawest is that great city, which
reigneth over the kings of the earth.
                                            —Revelation 17:18

Can the Book of Revelation be read as an exploration and
struggle for spiritual consciousness—your individual spiritual consciousness—rather than a blueprint for the imminent end of the
known world?

The Bible says it speaks to all people who ever read or hear it.
The Book reveals itself. The final book of the Bible, Revelation,
mirrors the struggle to accept individual spiritual revelation and to
put that spiritual revelation into daily practice. Revelation depicts,
in graphic imagery, a war between light and dark. "The Revelation
of Jesus Christ, which God gave unto him" (1:9–12) was given to
John, in exile, on the Greek island of Patmos. John writes the words
given to him directly by Jesus. The revelation is addressed to all servants of God without limitation as to time or place—it is to be a
book for all people for all time.

In Revelation 22:18–19, there is a stern warning that the text
is to stand as it is. As with the Commandments, it may not be
added to or subtracted from. Hence the book must be read not
selectively but as a whole. Summaries will not do justice to the
force, power, and message of Revelation. Given the nature of the
book, the best thing you can do is to read it for yourself and see
what it says to you. The sketch that follows may help the reader
with the overall structure of Revelation and a very, very few of the

themes expressed there, but it is no substitute for exploring the book for oneself.

Alpha and Omega

John hears Jesus say: "I am Alpha and Omega, the first and the last" (Revelation 1:10–11). This may be taken to mean the first "man" and the last "man"—that is, spiritual man present with God, Spirit, just as "in the beginning." Those interested in biblical numerology and symbols have a field day with Revelation. Further, the Word melds its literary sense with its mathematical sense. Some readers have felt that some sort of codebook to Revelation is an absolute necessity, or they have relied on other's interpretations.

One vision that John sees is of a lamb with seven horns and seven eyes standing in the center of a colored throne (Revelation 5:6). What at first glance might seem to be a hideous monster can be read as a symbol of the complete strength and understanding of The Creator and Creation. Jesus in his crucifixion is the Lamb. The seventh day is the day of completion in Creation. The horn is a symbol of strength, mentioned in Hannah's song (1 Samuel 2:1). Eyes represent sight and understanding. If we knew thoroughly the Books of Ezekiel and Daniel, the Gospel of John, procedural ritual in the temple, the Hebrew theory of numbers, and the uses of horn in previous Bible texts—as the people of John's time did—this revelation might not seem so obscure or difficult.

Seven Messages to the Churches

So many people study the book of Revelation in so many ways that any summary seems presumptuous. But as Isaiah has said, "come ye to the waters," and so we plunge ahead on our journey in very, very short form, remembering that the Bible is the most self-referential of all books. The Book of Revelation consists of seven visions, as there are seven days of Creation. The seven visions are stated in a prologue and epilogue. The prologue is a message to seven churches and divides into seven parts. The seven messages to the churches, in chapters 2 and 3, address the qualities and characteristics of individual behavior, contrasting the best in human behavior with the worst. *Church* is a word in feminine form.

1. In the first message, to the "church at Ephesus," she—the church—has intelligently tested all things for herself and she has shown hard work and patience. But she left her first love, either abandoning it or letting it weaken by not being as loving as she used to be. Unless she changes her thinking immediately upon hearing the analysis of her behavior, she will be in trouble and bereft. But if she does return to "her first works," she gets "the tree of life" that Adam and Eve missed (Revelation 2:1–7).

2. In the second message she claims that she is poor when she is really rich. But if she can remain faithful and overcome any misrepresentation of herself, she shall not miss resurrection (Revelation 2:8–11).

3. If she strives to overcome her struggles with idol worship and promiscuity, she will receive a new name, on a white stone— a name "which no man knoweth" (Revelation 2:12–17).

4. She is loving and faithful and has worked hard, but she allowed the woman Jezebel to teach and seduce. Whoever follows Jezebel will be destroyed. But the victor over Jezebel gets all power and "the morning star" (Revelation 2:18–28).

5. Her work isn't perfect in the sight of God. She has got to hold fast and repent and watch more carefully or everything will be taken from her. The victor over these stumbling blocks is to be "clothed in white raiment" and to hear her name spoken in the presence of God (Revelation 3:1–6).

6. She has an open door in front of her that "no man can shut," and she has used her talents to the full. Her task is to hold on

to this; if she does, she is "a pillar in the temple of God . . . in the city of . . . God . . . new Jerusalem" (Revelation 3:7–13).

7. She is lukewarm in her devotion and practice, and alternating between hot and cold. She has forgotten the poor and is very proud of herself and her position in the world, but she is loved anyway. She will be rebuked, but as rebuke and chastening are a sign of love, she shouldn't worry. She will be placed "on a throne of dominion in the lap of God" (Revelation 3:14–22).

What follows in Revelation is either a continuation of the experience of Jesus or the explication of a further vision of John about the experience of Jesus. There are varying schools of thought; one must decide for oneself.

Seven Visions

Revelation describes seven visions, which are the steps in the destruction of the darkness by the light as revealed in the beginning. These visions are elaborate, fantastic and grotesque to the modern mind, and they refer, directly and symbolically, to other parts of the Bible.

1. Revelation chapters 4 and 5: Everyone is happy because the "Lion of the tribe of Juda, the Root of David" has opened the book and demonstrated spiritual life. The truth about God is out.

2. Revelation chapter 6: The four horsemen emerge from the first four of seven seals, coming to wage war with the idea of the Creator. This vision illustrates that there is no absolute safety anywhere in the world—only in Spirit. When the seventh seal is opened there is silence for half an hour.

3. Revelation chapters 8 and 9: The silence is broken by seven trumpets. One-third of everything dies, but not everything—a reminder that there is always so much more left than is

taken away. A book is presented in Revelation 10:9 as it is in Ezekiel 3:3, "sweet as honey in the mouth but bitter in the belly." The good news about God is out, but it doesn't settle very well. The female is coming into her rightful place, and this causes upheaval. The fourth vision appears only after a description of the resurrection of two witnesses.

4. Revelation chapters 12–14: "And there appeared a great wonder in heaven; a woman clothed with the sun, and the moon under her feet, and upon her head a crown of twelve stars." She is pregnant "and she being with child cried, travailing in birth, and pained to be delivered." Menacing her is a great red dragon, the snake from Eden grown large. The dragon is waiting to devour her child as soon as it is born. "And she brought forth a man child, who was to rule all nations with a rod of iron; and her child was caught up unto God, and to his throne." The woman fled into the wilderness, where her "place was already prepared by God," and she is nourished there. Then there is war, "and Michael and his angels fought against the dragon and the dragon was cast out, that old serpent, called the Devil, and Satan, which deceiveth the whole world; he was cast out into the earth. . . . When the dragon saw that he was cast to the earth he persecuted the woman." And again the woman is saved.

She is given "two wings of a great eagle, to fly into her place in the wilderness where she is nourished for a time, and times, and a time, from the face of the serpent." Here again are the eagle's wings, on which God said in Deuteronomy, "I have borne you up."

But the dragon tries to give authority to a terrible beast: "And that no one might buy or sell save he that had the mark, or the name of the beast, or the number of his name." This number is 666, which some readers suggest means three attempts to reach seven and three failures. Chapter 14 is a contrast to chapter 13. John sees a Lamb standing on Mount

Zion and 144,000 with him who have his Father's name on their foreheads. "These are they which have not defiled women: for they are virgins. . . ." Were one to read these verses literally, one might say that only celibate males are to be saved. That interpretation would be at odds with the Holy Scripture that has gone before and is yet to come in Revelation. One might surmise the meaning here to be in the area of purity—no intercourse or communication with the false Jezebel who kills prophets and her own children.

5. Revelation chapters 15–18: The war gets worse. Seven plagues arrive, destroying any desire to worship the beast. For the first and only time in the Bible the place called Armageddon is mentioned: "And he gathered them together into a place called in the Hebrew tongue Armageddon." It's a masculine noun, a place name referring to mountains or rising up, and means "mountains of Meggido."

    In chapter 17 a woman appears on a scarlet beast. She is opposite to the woman with "the twelve stars on her crown"— the woman who represents the Motherhood of God. The woman on the beast, on the other hand, is "MYSTERY, BABYLON THE GREAT, THE MOTHER OF HARLOTS AND ABOMINATIONS OF THE EARTH."

    Why mystery? Perhaps it suggests that evil is fundamentally abstruse—dark, not light. The woman, Babylon, is destroyed and with her all endeavors that do not flow from God.

6. Revelation chapters 19 and 20: A rider appears on a white horse, followed by the armies of heaven. Out of the rider's mouth comes a sharp sword (as in the sword that protects the tree of life in Eden). And everything that does not come from God is cast into the lake of fire.

7. Revelation chapters 21 and 22: The old heaven and earth are gone, replaced with new ones as Isaiah 65 and 66 prophesied.

And "the new heaven and new earth"—this new, purified by purgation sense of Life—is represented as a reuniting of male and female from Genesis 1:27. *Ruah Elohim* has moved on the face of the waters of all consciousness, history, all life, all men and women, and, in male and female symbols of utmost purity, we read of the "holy city prepared as a bride adorned for her husband."

John describes it:

> And I saw a new heaven and a new earth: for the first heaven and the first earth were passed away; and there was no more sea.
>
> And I John saw the holy city, new Jerusalem, coming down from God out of heaven, prepared as a bride adorned for her husband.
>
> And I heard a great voice out of heaven saying, Behold, the tabernacle of God is with men, and he will dwell with them, and they shall be his people, and God himself shall be with them, and be their God.
>
> And God shall wipe away all tears from their eyes; and there shall be no more death, neither sorrow, nor crying, neither shall there be any more pain: for the former things are passed away. (Revelation 21:1–4)

There will be no more crying, sorrow, death or pain, because all that was associated with the curse on Eve is gone. Revelation 22:3 says: "And there shall be no more curse. Behold, I make all things new." The visions are over, indicated by the repetition of "I am Alpha and Omega, the beginning and the end" (21:6, 22:13).

The heavenly city has "no need of the sun, neither of the moon" (Revelation 21:3), but is lit by the glory of God, as in Creation where there was light before the sun or moon. *Glory* here is a feminine noun with a definition: "splendor, brightness of the moon, sun, stars, magnificence, excellence, preeminence, dignity, grace, majesty."

The struggle is at an end. The destruction of the dark by the Light is complete. The consciousness of the children of Light is brought into focus in graphic imagery. The children of Israel, those who strive with God, have seen the cloud and the glory, fought the fight, dwelt among the heathen, gone repeatedly astray, dwelt with conscious awareness of the Law and the Prophets, and sojourned with women and men who live, love, come to terms with their heritage, and receive the Revelation.

Revelation 22 promises a reward to anyone who has made it though the struggle to recognize the Power, Allness, and Goodness of God, the Omnipresence and Omniscience of the God who has many names but is One. Anyone who can and has made it through the deceptions, the terrible beasts, and the horrors that lie on the path to the holy city will be rewarded with the right to the tree of life.

In the beginning of the Bible we read of two creations. One account (Genesis 1) records eternity, the other (Genesis 2) chronological time. After the two accounts have been laid out, we see evidences of both kinds of time separate and intersecting. Narratives periodically give way, the mist of the second creation parts to reveal the eternal, the spiritual, the face and voice, the understanding of the presence and power of Spirit in the flesh and the daily affairs of all.

In Revelation the two stories have become one story. We have reached Eden, but without the curse, without the serpent, without any deceit. The male and female are one again as they were in the beginning. The Spirit joins with the bride to say, "Come. Anyone who will can take of the water of life freely."

As in the beginning, *ruah Elohim* moves on the face of those waters.

Bibliography

Bibles

The Bible: An American translation. J. M. Powis Smith (Ed., Old Testament) and Edgar J. Goodspeed (Ed., New Testament). The University of Chicago Press, 1935.

The Bible for today's family: Contemporary English version. New Testament. Thomas Nelson Publishers, 1991.

The Good News Bible: The Bible in today's English version. American Bible Society, 1971, 1976.

The Holy Bible containing the Old and New Testaments: Translated out of the original tongues; And with the former translations diligently compared and revised, by His Majesty's special command: Authorized King James Version. Cambridge at the University Press.

Holy Bible: New revised standard version. American Bible Society, 1989.

The message: The Bible in contemporary language. (Eugene H. Peterson, Trans.). NavPress, 2002.

The New Testament in modern English. (J. B. Phillips, Trans.). The Macmillan Company, 1958.

Tanakh—The Holy Scriptures: The new JPS translation according to the traditional Hebrew text. The Jewish Publication Society, 1985.

The Torah: A modern commentary. W. Gunther Plaut (Ed.). Union of American Hebrew Congregations. New York, 1981.

Tyndale's Old Testament: Being the Pentateuch of 1530, Joshua to 2 Chronicles of 1537 and Jonah. (William Tyndale, Trans.). In the modern spelling edition and with an introduction by David Daniell. Yale University Press, 1992. (Forms the basis of the King James Version; translated by Tyndale directly from the Hebrew in 1530, five years before he was executed for his zeal and translation efforts and three decades before verses were installed by printer Robert Etienne.)

www.crosswalk.com: Twenty-seven versions of the Bible online with study aids.

Study Aids

Geseniums, H.W.F. (1979). *Gesenius' Hebrew-Chaldee lexicon to the Old Testament*. Grand Rapids, MI: Baker Book House.

Strong, James, S.T.D., LL.D. (1890/1987). *Strong's exhaustive concordance*. Grand Rapids, MI: Baker Book House.

Thayer, Joseph H. (1977). *Thayer's Greek-English lexicon of the New Testament*. Grand Rapids, MI: Baker Book House.

Selected Sources

Alter, Robert. (1981). *The art of biblical narrative*. New York: Basic Books.

Alter, Robert. (1999). *The David story: A translation with commentary of 1 and 2 Samuel*. New York and London: Norton.

Alter, Robert. (2004). *The five books of Moses: A translation with commentary*. New York: Norton.

Auerbach, Eric. (1952). *Mimesis: The representation of reality in western literature*. Princeton, NJ: Princeton University Press.

Austin, Mary. (1912). *Christ in Italy: Being the adventures of a maverick among masterpieces*. New York: Duffield.

Bal, Mieke. (1998). *Death and dissymmetry: The politics of coherence in the book of Judges*. Chicago and London: University of Chicago Press.

Buber, Martin. (1968). *On the Bible: Eighteen studies*. New York: Schocken Books.

Carmody, Denise Lardner. (1988). *Biblical woman: Contemporary reflections on spiritual texts*. New York: Crossroad.

Chase, Mary Ellen. (1944). *The Bible and the common reader*. New York: Macmillan.

Chute, Marchette. (1947). *The end of the search*. Harrington Park, NJ: Sommer.

Chute, Marchette. (1969). *The search for God*. Harrington Park, NJ: Sommer.

Croatto, J. Severion. (1984). *Biblical hermeneutics*. (Robert R. Barr, Trans.). Maryknoll, NY: Orbis Books.

Currid, John D. (1997). *Ancient Egypt and the Old Testament*. Grand Rapids, MI: Baker Books.

Curzon, David. (1995). *The gospels in our image: An anthology of twentieth-century poetry based on biblical texts*. New York: Harcourt Brace.

Deen, Edith. (1955). *All the women of the Bible*. New York: HarperCollins.

Eddy, Mary Baker. (1875). *Science and health with key to the scriptures*. Boston: Christian Science Publishing Society.

Frye, Northrup. (1992). *The great code: The Bible in literature*. New York: Free Press.

Girard, Rene. (1977). *Violence and the sacred*. (Patrick Gregory, Trans.). Baltimore: Johns Hopkins University Press.

Girard, Rene. (1986). *The scapegoat*. (Yvonne Freccero, Trans.). Baltimore: Johns Hopkins University Press.

Green, Arthur (Ed.). (1987). *Jewish spirituality: From the Bible through the Middle Ages*. New York: Crossroad.

Grosz, Elizabeth. (1989). *Sexual subversions*: Sydney: Allen and Unwin.

Hendel, Ronald. (2005). *Remembering Abraham: Culture, memory, and history in the Hebrew Bible*. Oxford, UK: Oxford University Press.

James, William. (1961). *The varieties of religious experience*. New York: Macmillan. (Original work published 1902)

Josipivici, Gabriel. (1988). *The book of God: A response to the Bible*. New Haven and London: Yale University Press.

Kermode, Frank. (1979). *The genesis of secrecy: On the interpretation of narrative*. Cambridge, MA, and London: Harvard University Press.

Lassner, Jacob. (1993). *Demonizing the Queen of Sheba: Boundaries of gender and culture in postbiblical Judaism and medieval Islam*. Chicago and London: University of Chicago Press.

Luther, Martin. (1988). *Martin Luther: Selections from his writings*. John Dillenberger (Ed.). New York: Knopf.

Mann, Thomas. (1988). *Joseph and his brothers* (15th ed.). (H. T. Lowe-Porter, Trans.). New York: Knopf.

Mozeson, Isaac E. (1989). *The word: The dictionary that reveals the Hebrew source of English*. New York: Shapolsky Publishers.

Nicolson, Adam. (2003). *God's secretaries: The making of the King James Bible*. New York: Harper: Perennial.

Pinsky, Robert. (2005). *The life of David*. New York: Nextbook Schocken.

Plaskow, Judith. (1990). *Standing again at Sinai: Judaism from a feminist perspective*. San Francisco: HarperSanFrancisco.

Preminger, Alex, and Greenstein, Edward L. (Compilers and Eds.). (1986). *The Hebrew Bible in literary criticism*. New York: Ungar.

Renckens, H. (1964). *Israel's concept of the beginning: The theology of Genesis 1–111*. New York: Herder and Herder.

Rose, Jacqueline. (1986). *Sexuality in the field of vision*. London: Verso.

Sacks, Robert. (2003). *The book of Job with commentary: A translation for our time*. University of South Florida Press.

Schafer, Peter. (2003). *Mirror of His beauty: Feminine images of God from the Bible to the early Kabbalah*. Princeton and London: Princeton University Press.

Schwartz, Regina (Ed.). (1990). *The Book and the text: The Bible and literary theory*. Cambridge, MA: Blackwell.

Stowe, Harriet Beecher. (1873/1990). *Women in sacred history: A celebration of women in the Bible*. New York: Portland House.

Sweeney, Marvin. (2001). *King Josiah of Judah: The Lost Messiah of Israel*. New York: Oxford University Press.

Trible, Phyllis. (1978). *God and the rhetoric of sexuality*. Minneapolis: Augsberg Fortress.

———. (1984). *Texts of terror: Literary-feminist readings of biblical narratives*. Minneapolis: Augsberg Fortress.

The Author

Lynne Bundesen is the author of *So the Woman Went Her Way* and *One Prayer at a Time*. She has served as an adjunct professor at the Boston Theological Institute under a Templeton Science and Religion grant and was manager of the Microsoft Network Religion Community. Bundesen is a three-time winner of the Religion in Media Award for her syndicated column on religion. She is currently the spiritual expert for the physical and spiritual health Web site of Dr. Andrew Weil and a columnist for religionandspirituality.com.